Swift Protocol-Oriented Programming
Fourth Edition

Increase productivity and build faster applications with Swift 5

Jon Hoffman

BIRMINGHAM - MUMBAI

Contributors

About the author

Jon Hoffman has over 20 years' experience in the field of Information Technology. Over those 20 years, Jon has worked in the system administration, network administration, network security, application development, and architecture arenas. Currently, he works as an Enterprise Software Manager at Syntech Systems. He has developed extensively for the iOS platform since 2008. This includes several apps that he has published in the App Store, apps that he has written for third parties, and numerous enterprise applications. Some of Jon's other interests are playing basketball, kayaking, and working out with his daughters. Jon also really enjoys Tae Kwon Do, where he and his oldest daughter earned their black belts together early in 2014 and are currently 3rd-degree Black Belts.

> *With this being the fourth edition of this book, I would like to thank everyone that has given me encouragement, positive feedback, and constructive criticism though the years. That includes family, friends, co-workers, and everyone at Packt.*

About the reviewers

Nikola Brežnjak is an engineer at heart and a jack of all trades. Currently, he's the director of engineering at Teltech, where he is responsible for the management, mentoring, and coaching of mobile app developers. He loves his job! He has written books on the Ionic framework and the MEAN stack, and has been a technical reviewer for a number of Packt books. He likes to help out on Stack Overflow, where he's a top contributor. He records a podcast called DevThink with his friend, Shawn Milochik, and runs a local meetup called MeCoDe.

> *I would like to thank my wife for supporting me in all my geeky endeavors and my parents for teaching me the power of hard and consistent work.*

Vinod Madigeri is a senior software engineer with expertise in full-stack app development. He received his master's in computer science from the University of Utah in 2015. He has worked in several industries (telecommunications, game technologies, and consumer electronics) as a developer, team leader, and mentor, writing software—in C, C++, Python, Objective-C, and Swift—for macOS and iOS platforms.

Currently, he spends much of his time exploring machine learning as a skill to complement his software development efforts.

Vinod has also been a technical reviewer for *Mastering Swift 5*, *Object–Oriented Programming with Swift*, *Hands-On Full-Stack Development with Swift*, and *Multiplayer Game Development with HTML5*.

> *I'd like to thank my wife, Shruti, for her constant support, encouragement, and vanguard thoughts.*

Packt is searching for authors like you

If you're interested in becoming an author for Packt, please visit `authors.packtpub.com` and apply today. We have worked with thousands of developers and tech professionals, just like you, to help them share their insight with the global tech community. You can make a general application, apply for a specific hot topic that we are recruiting an author for, or submit your own idea.

Table of Contents

Preface

Apple announced Swift 2 at the **World Wide Developers Conference** (**WWDC**) in 2015. They also declared that Swift was the world's first protocol-oriented programming language. Judging by the name, someone might assume that protocol-oriented programming is all about the protocol or is simply object-oriented programming under a different name. These assumptions would be wrong. Protocol-oriented programming is about so much more than just the protocol; it is actually a new way of not only writing applications but thinking about the design of our application.

In the first five chapters of this book, we take an in-depth look at each of the components of the protocol-oriented programming paradigm. These chapters are designed to give you a solid understanding of the different components of protocol-oriented programming, so that you can understand how to use these components in your applications. One of the biggest misconceptions about protocol-oriented programming is that it is just another name for object-oriented programming. In Chapter 6, *Object-Oriented Programming*, and Chapter 7, *Protocol-Oriented Programming*, we take on this myth by comparing protocol-oriented programming to object-oriented programming to see what is similar and what is different. We also discuss the advantages and disadvantages of both programming paradigms.

The last two chapters are written to help you understand how you can design your application in a protocol-oriented programming way. Chapter 8, *Adopting Design Patterns in Swift*, looks at how we can implement several design patterns in a protocol-oriented way, and Chapter 9, *Case Studies*, looks at three real-world case studies to reinforce everything previously discussed in the book.

Who this book is for

This book is intended for the developer who has at least an introductory knowledge of the Swift programming language and wants to understand what protocol-oriented programming is. This book is written for the developer who not only wants to understand protocol-oriented programming but also wants to fully understand the different components of the programming paradigm. This book is written for the developer who learns best by looking at and working with code, because every concept covered in the book is backed by example code written to give you a solid understanding of the current topic and to demonstrate how to properly implement it.

What this book covers

Chapter 1, *Starting with the Protocol*, looks at what protocols are and how they are used in the Swift programming language. We will also examine how protocols can be used to write very flexible and reusable code.

Chapter 2, *Our Type Choices*, discusses the different types that Swift offers (structs, classes, enums, and tuples). We will look at several examples of when to use the various types and when not to.

Chapter 3, *Extensions*, looks at how extensions and protocol extensions are used with the Swift programming language. We will look at examples of how extensions can be used with protocol-oriented programming.

Chapter 4, *Generics*, shows how powerful generics are. Apple has stated that Generics are one of the most powerful features of Swift. We will look at how to use Generics to make very flexible types, and also how to implement the **Copy-on-Write (COW)** feature for our custom types.

Chapter 5, *Memory Management*, looks at how Swift manages memory with **Automatic Reference Counting (ARC)** and how strong reference cycles can cause ARC to fail. We also look at how to use weak and unowned references.

Chapter 6, *Object-Oriented Programming*, examines how we would develop characters for a video game if we were taking an object-oriented approach. In order to really appreciate the ideas behind protocol-oriented programming, we need to understand the problems it is designed to solve. We will then look at the drawbacks with this design.

Chapter 7, *Protocol-Oriented Programming*, develops the same video game characters from Chapter 5, *Memory Management*, but this time we will take a protocol-oriented approach to the design. We will then compare the object-oriented approach and the protocol-oriented approach to see the advantages that the protocol-oriented approach offers.

Chapter 8, *Adopting Design Patterns in Swift*, looks at implementing several design patterns using protocol-oriented programming. For each of the design patterns, we will look at the problem they are designed to solve and how to implement the pattern.

Chapter 9, *Case Studies*, explores two case studies. This chapter is designed to pull everything from the first six chapters together to show you how to use protocol-oriented programming in real-world situations.

To get the most out of this book

To follow along with the examples in this book, you will need to have an Apple computer with OS X 10.14 or higher installed. You will also need to install Xcode version 10.2 or higher with Swift version 5 or higher. You should possess at least a basic knowledge of the Swift programming language and how to use the development tools on their environment.

Download the example code files

You can download the example code files for this book from your account at `www.packt.com`. If you purchased this book elsewhere, you can visit `www.packt.com/support` and register to have the files emailed directly to you.

You can download the code files by following these steps:

1. Log in or register at `www.packt.com`.
2. Select the **SUPPORT** tab.
3. Click on **Code Downloads & Errata**.
4. Enter the name of the book in the **Search** box and follow the onscreen instructions.

Once the file is downloaded, please make sure that you unzip or extract the folder using the latest version of:

- WinRAR/7-Zip for Windows
- Zipeg/iZip/UnRarX for Mac
- 7-Zip/PeaZip for Linux

The code bundle for the book is also hosted on GitHub at `https://github.com/PacktPublishing/Swift-5-Protocol-Oriented-Programming-Fourth-Edition`. In case there's an update to the code, it will be updated on the existing GitHub repository.

We also have other code bundles from our rich catalog of books and videos available at `https://github.com/PacktPublishing/`. Check them out!

Conventions used

There are a number of text conventions used throughout this book.

`CodeInText`: Indicates code words in text, database table names, folder names, filenames, file extensions, pathnames, dummy URLs, user input, and Twitter handles. Here is an example: "To define the protocol, we use the `protocol` keyword, followed by the name of the protocol."

A block of code is set as follows:

```
struct  MyStruct:  MyProtocol  {
    //Structure  implementation  here
}
```

When we wish to draw your attention to a particular part of a code block, the relevant lines or items are set in bold:

```
Initializing class with name One
Initializing class with name Two
Setting class1ref1 to nil
Releaseing class with name One
Setting class2ref1 to nil
Setting class2ref2 to nil
Releaseing class with name Two
```

Bold: Indicates a new term, an important word, or words that you see onscreen. For example, words in menus or dialog boxes appear in the text like this. Here is an example: "If we run this example, we will see that the **Notification Received** message."

 Warnings or important notes appear like this.

 Tips and tricks appear like this.

Get in touch

Feedback from our readers is always welcome.

General feedback: If you have questions about any aspect of this book, mention the book title in the subject of your message and email us at `customercare@packtpub.com`.

Errata: Although we have taken every care to ensure the accuracy of our content, mistakes do happen. If you have found a mistake in this book, we would be grateful if you would report this to us. Please visit www.packt.com/submit-errata, selecting your book, clicking on the Errata Submission Form link, and entering the details.

Piracy: If you come across any illegal copies of our works in any form on the Internet, we would be grateful if you would provide us with the location address or website name. Please contact us at copyright@packt.com with a link to the material.

If you are interested in becoming an author: If there is a topic that you have expertise in and you are interested in either writing or contributing to a book, please visit authors.packtpub.com.

Reviews

Please leave a review. Once you have read and used this book, why not leave a review on the site that you purchased it from? Potential readers can then see and use your unbiased opinion to make purchase decisions, we at Packt can understand what you think about our products, and our authors can see your feedback on their book. Thank you!

For more information about Packt, please visit packt.com.

1
Starting with the Protocol

This book is all about protocol-oriented programming. When Apple announced Swift 2 at the **World Wide Developers Conference (WWDC)** in 2015, they also declared that Swift was the world's first protocol-oriented programming language. From its name, we may assume that protocol-oriented programming is all about the protocol; however, this would be incorrect. Protocol-oriented programming is about so much more than just the protocol; it's actually a new way of not only writing applications, but also how we think about application design.

In this chapter, you will learn about the following topics:

- How to define property and functional requirements within a protocol
- How to use protocol inheritance and composition
- How to use a protocol as a type
- What is polymorphism?
- How to use associated types with protocols
- How to implement the delegation pattern with protocols
- How to design type requirements with protocols

If you are coming from an object-oriented programming background, you may be familiar with the interface. In the object-oriented world, for most languages, the interface is a type that contains method and property signatures but does not contain implementation details. An interface can be considered a contract where any type that conforms to the interface must implement the required functionality defined within it. Most object-oriented developers rarely use interfaces as the focal point for their application design unless they are working with a framework similar to the **Open Service Gateway Initiative (OSGi)** framework. In protocol-oriented programming, the protocol is the focal point of your design.

When we are designing an application in an object-oriented way, we usually begin by focusing on the class hierarchy and how the objects interact. The object is a data structure that contains information about the attributes of the object in the form of properties, and the actions performed by or to the object in the form of methods. We cannot create an object without a blueprint that tells the application what attributes and actions to expect from the object. In most object-oriented languages, this blueprint comes in the form of a class. A class is a construct that allows us to encapsulate the properties and actions of an object into a single type.

Designing an application in a protocol-oriented way is significantly different from designing it in an object-oriented way. Rather than starting with the class hierarchy, protocol-oriented design says that we should start with the protocol. While protocol-oriented design is about so much more than just the protocol, we can think of the protocol as its backbone. After all, it would be pretty hard to have protocol-oriented programming without the protocol.

A protocol in Swift is similar to the interface in object-oriented languages, where the protocol acts as a contract that defines the methods, properties, and other requirements that are needed by our types to perform their tasks. We say that the protocol acts as a contract because any type that conforms to the protocol promises to implement the requirements defined by the protocol itself. If a type says that it conforms to a protocol and it doesn't implement all the functionality defined by the protocol, we will get a compile-time error and the project will not compile. In Swift, any class, structure, or enumeration can conform to a protocol.

We've just mentioned that the protocol is similar to the interface. Don't be fooled by this comparison because even though the interface and the protocol are similar, protocols in Swift are actually far more powerful than the interface in most object-oriented languages. As you read this book, you will find out how powerful Swift protocols can be.

Most modern object-oriented programming languages implement their standard library with a class hierarchy; however, the basis of Swift's standard library is the protocol (`http://swiftdoc.org`). Therefore, not only does Apple recommend that we use the protocol-oriented programming paradigm in our applications, but to also use it in the Swift standard library.

With the protocol being the basis of the Swift standard library and also the backbone of the protocol-oriented programming paradigm, it is very important that we fully understand what the protocol is and how we can use it. In this chapter, we will cover not only the basics of the protocol but also provide an understanding on how it can be used in application design.

Protocol syntax

In this section, we will look at how to define a protocol and how to add requirements to it. This will give us a basic understanding of the protocol. The rest of this chapter will build on this understanding.

Defining a protocol

The syntax we use to define a protocol is very similar to the syntax that's used to define a class, structure, or enumeration. The following example shows the syntax that's used to define a protocol:

```
protocol MyProtocol {
    //protocol definition here
}
```

To define the protocol, we use the `protocol` keyword, followed by the name of the protocol. We then put the requirements, which our protocol defines, between curly brackets. Custom types can state that they conform to a particular protocol by placing the name of the protocol after the type's name, separated by a colon. The following example shows how we would define that a structure conforms to a protocol:

```
struct  MyStruct:  MyProtocol  {
    //Structure  implementation  here
}
```

A type can also conform to multiple protocols. We list the multiple protocols that the type conforms to by separating them with commas:

```
struct MyStruct: MyProtocol, AnotherProtocol, ThirdProtocol {
    //Structure implementation here
}
```

Having a type conform to multiple protocols is a very important concept within protocol-oriented programming, as we will see later in this chapter and throughout this book. This concept is known as protocol composition. Now, let's see how we would add property requirements to our protocol.

Property requirements

A protocol can require that the conforming types provide certain properties with specified names and types. The protocol doesn't say whether the property should be a stored or computed property because the implementation details are left up to the conforming types.

When defining a property within a protocol, we must specify whether the property is a read-only or a read-write property by using the `get` and `set` keywords. We also need to specify the property's type since we cannot use type inference in a protocol. Let's look at how we would define properties within a protocol by creating a protocol named `FullName`, as shown in the following example:

```
protocol FullName {
    var firstName: String {get  set}
    var lastName: String {get  set}
}
```

In this example, we define two properties named `firstName` and `lastName`, which are read-write properties. Any type that conforms to this protocol must implement both of these properties. If we wanted to define the property as read-only, we would define it using only the `get` keyword, as shown in the following code:

```
var readOnly: String {get}
```

It is possible to define static properties by using the `static` keyword, as shown in the following example:

```
static var typeProperty: String {get}
```

Static properties are properties that are owned by the type and shared by all instances. This means that if one instance changes the value of this property, then the value changes for all instances. We will look at how to use static instances more when we look at the singleton pattern.

Now, let's look at how we would add method requirements to our protocol.

Method requirements

A protocol can require that the conforming types provide specific methods. These methods are defined within the protocol exactly as we define them within a class or structure, but without the curly brackets and method body. We can define that these methods are instance or type methods using the `static` keyword. Adding default values to the method's parameters is not allowed when defining the method within a protocol.

Let's add a method named `getFullName()` to the `FullName` protocol:

```
protocol FullName  {
    var firstName: String {get  set}
    var lastName: String {get  set}

    func getFullName() -> String
}
```

The `FullName` protocol now requires one method named `getFullName()` and two read-write properties named `firstName` and `lastName`.

For value types, such as the structure, if we intend for a method to modify the instances that it belongs to, we must prefix the method definition with the `mutating` keyword. This keyword indicates that the method is allowed to modify the instance it belongs to. The following example shows how to use the `mutating` keyword with a method definition:

```
mutating func changeName()
```

If we mark a method requirement as mutating, we don't need to write the `mutating` keyword for that method when we adopt the protocol with a reference (class) type. The `mutating` keyword is only used with value (structures or enumerations) types.

Optional requirements

There are times when we want protocols to define optional requirements. An optional requirement is a method or property that doesn't need to be implemented. To use optional requirements, we need to start off by marking the protocol with the `@objc` attribute.

 It is important to note that only classes can adopt protocols that use the `@objc` attribute. Structures and enumerations cannot adopt these protocols.

To mark a property or method as optional, we use the `optional` keyword. The following example shows how we would create both an `optional` property and also an `optional` method:

```
@objc protocol Phone {
    var phoneNumber: String {get  set}
    @objc optional var emailAddress: String {get  set}
    func dialNumber()
    @objc optional func getEmail()
}
```

If we are using the `@objc` attribute, as shown in the previous example, we cannot use the `mutating` keyword because it isn't valid for classes. Now, let's explore how protocol inheritance works.

Protocol inheritance

Protocols can inherit requirements from one or more additional protocols and then add additional requirements. The following code shows the syntax for protocol inheritance:

```
protocol ProtocolThree: ProtocolOne, ProtocolTwo {
    //Add requirements here
}
```

The syntax for protocol inheritance is very similar to class inheritance in Swift, except that we are able to inherit from more than one protocol. Let's see how protocol inheritance works. We will use the `FullName` protocol that we defined earlier and create a new protocol named `Person`:

```
protocol Person: FullName {
    var age: Int {get set}
}
```

Now, when we create a type that conforms to the `Person` protocol, we must implement the requirements defined in the `Person` protocol, as well as the requirements defined in the `FullName` protocol. As an example, we could define a `Student` structure that conforms to the `Person` protocol, as shown in the following code:

```
struct Student: Person {
    var firstName = ""
    var lastName = ""
    var age = 0

    func getFullName() -> String {
        return "\(firstName) \(lastName)"
    }
}
```

Note that in the `Student` structure, we implemented the requirements defined in both the `FullName` and `Person` protocols. However, the only protocol specified in the structure definition was the `Person` protocol. We only needed to list the `Person` protocol because it inherited all the requirements from the `FullName` protocol.

Now, let's look at a very important concept in the protocol-oriented programming paradigm: *protocol composition*.

Protocol composition

Protocol composition lets our types adopt multiple protocols. This is a major advantage that we get when we use protocols rather than a class hierarchy because classes, in Swift and other single-inheritance languages, can only inherit from one superclass. The syntax for protocol composition is the same as the syntax for protocol inheritance that we just saw. The following example shows how we would use protocol composition:

```
struct MyStruct: ProtocolOne, ProtocolTwo, Protocolthree {
    //implementation  here
}
```

Protocol composition allows us to break our requirements into many smaller components rather than inheriting all the requirements from a single protocol or single superclass. This allows our type families to grow in width rather than height, which means we avoid creating bloated types that contain requirements that are not needed by all conforming types. Protocol composition may seem like a very simple concept, but it is a concept that is essential to protocol-oriented programming. Let's look at an example of protocol composition so that we can see the advantage we get from using it.

Let's say that we have the class hierarchy that's shown in the following diagram:

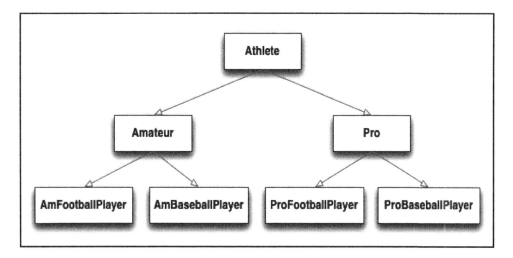

In this class hierarchy, we have a base class named **Athlete**. The **Athlete** base class then has two subclasses named **Amateur** and **Pro**. These classes are used depending on whether the athlete is an amateur athlete or a pro athlete. An amateur athlete may be a collegiate athlete, and we would need to store information such as which school they go to and their GPA. A pro athlete is one that gets paid for playing the game. For the pro athletes, we would need to store information such as what team they play for and their salary.

In this example, things get a little messy under the **Amateur** and **Pro** classes. As we can see, we have separate football player classes under both the **Amateur** and **Pro** classes (the **AmFootballPlayer** and **ProFootballPlayer** classes). We also have separate baseball classes under both the **Amateur** and **Pro** classes (the **AmBaseballPlayer** and **ProBaseballPlayer** classes). This means we need to have a lot of duplicate code between these classes.

With protocol composition, instead of having a class hierarchy where our subclasses inherit all the functionality from a single superclass, we have a collection of protocols that we can mix and match in our types:

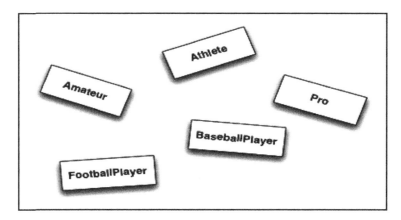

We can then use one or more of these protocols as needed for our types. For example, we can create an **AmFootballPlayer** structure that conforms to the **Athlete**, **Amateur**, and **FootballPlayer** protocols. We could then create the **ProFootballPlayer** structure that conforms to the **Athlete**, **Pro**, and **FootballPlayer** protocols. This allows us to be very specific about the requirements for our types and only adopt the requirements that we need.

From a pure protocol point of view, this example may not make a lot of sense right now because protocols only define the requirements; however, in Chapter 3, *Extensions*, we will look at how protocol extensions can be used to implement these types with minimal duplicate code.

One word of warning: if you find yourself creating numerous protocols that only contain one or two requirements in them, then you are probably making your protocols too granular. This will lead to a design that is hard to maintain and manage.

Now, let's look at how a protocol is a full-fledged type in Swift.

Using protocols as a type

Even though no functionality is implemented in a protocol, they are still considered a full-fledged type in the Swift programming language, and can mostly be used like any other type. What this means is that we can use protocols as parameters or return types for a function. We can also use them as the type for variables, constants, and collections. Let's look at some examples of this. For the next few examples, we will use the following Person protocol:

```
protocol Person {
    var firstName: String {get set}
    var lastName: String {get set}
    var birthDate: Date {get set}
    var profession: String {get}
    init (firstName: String, lastName: String, birthDate: Date)
}
```

In this Person protocol, we define four properties and one initializer.

For this first example, we will show you how to use a protocol as a parameter and return type for a function, method, or initializer. Within the function itself, we also use Person as the type for a variable:

```
func updatePerson(person: Person) -> Person  {
    var newPerson: Person
    // Code to update person goes here
    return newPerson
}
```

We can also use protocols as the type to store in a collection, as shown in the following example:

```
var personArray = [Person]()
var personDict = [String:  Person]()
```

We can use the instance of any type that conforms to our protocol anywhere that the protocol type is required. Let's assume that we have two types named `SwiftProgrammer` and `FootballPlayer` that conform to the `Person` protocol. We can then use them as follows:

```
var myPerson: Person

myPerson = SwiftProgrammer(firstName: "Jon", lastName: "Hoffman",
                              birthDate: birthDateProgrammer)
myPerson = FootballPlayer(firstName: "Dan", lastName: "Marino",
                              birthdate: birthDatePlayer)
```

As we saw earlier, we can use the `Person` protocol as the type for an array, which means that we can populate the array with instances of any type that conforms to the `Person` protocol. The following is an example of this (note that the `bDateProgrammer` and `bDatePlayer` variables are instances of the date type that would represent the birth date of the individual):

```
var programmer = SwiftProgrammer(firstName: "Jon", lastName: "Hoffman",
                                  birthDate:  bDateProgrammer)

var player = FootballPlayer(firstName: "Dan", lastName: "Marino",
                                  birthDate: bDatePlayer)

var people: [Person] = []
people.append(programmer)
people.append(player)
```

What we are seeing in these last couple of examples is a form of polymorphism. To use protocols to their fullest potential, we need to understand what polymorphism is.

Polymorphism with protocols

The word polymorphism comes from the Greek roots *poly* (meaning many) and *morphe* (meaning form). In programming languages, polymorphism is a single interface for multiple types (many forms). There are two reasons to learn the meaning of the word polymorphism. The first reason is that using such a fancy word can make you sound very intelligent in casual conversation. The second reason is that polymorphism provides one of the most useful programming techniques – not only in object-oriented programming, but also in protocol-oriented programming.

Polymorphism lets us interact with multiple types through a single uniform interface. In the object-oriented programming world, the single uniform interface usually comes from a superclass, while in the protocol-oriented programming world, that single interface usually comes from a protocol.

In the previous section, we saw two examples of polymorphism with Swift. The first example was as follows:

```
var myPerson: Person

myPerson = SwiftProgrammer(firstName: "Jon", lastName: "Hoffman",
                    birthDate: birthDateProgrammer)
myPerson = FootballPlayer(firstName: "Dan", lastName: "Marino",
                    birthdate: birthDatePlayer)
```

In this example, we had a single variable of the `Person` type. Polymorphism allowed us to set the variable to instances of any type that conforms to the `Person` protocol, such as the `SwiftProgrammer` or `FootballPlayer` types.

The other example of polymorphism was as follows:

```
var programmer = SwiftProgrammer(firstName: "Jon", lastName:  "Hoffman",
                    birthDate: bDateProgrammer)

var player = FootballPlayer(firstName: "Dan", lastName: "Marino",
                    birthDate: bDatePlayer)

var people: [Person] = []
people.append(programmer) people.append(player)
```

In this example, we created an array of `Person` types. Polymorphism allowed us to add instances of any types that conform to the `Person` protocol to this array.

When we access an instance of a type through a single uniform interface, as we just saw, we are unable to access type-specific functionality. As an example, if we had a property in the `FootballPlayer` type that records the age of the player, we would be unable to access that property because it is not defined in the `People` protocol.

If we do need to access type-specific functionality, we can use type casting.

Type casting with protocols

Type casting is a way to check the type of an instance and/or to treat the instance as a specified type. In Swift, we use the `is` keyword to check whether an instance is of a specific type and the `as` keyword to treat an instance as a specific type.

The following example shows how we would use the `is` keyword:

```
if person is SwiftProgrammer {
    print("(person.firstName) is a Swift Programmer")
}
```

In this example, the conditional statement returns true if the `Person` instance is of the `SwiftProgrammer` type, or false if it isn't. We can use the `where` statement in combination with the `is` keyword to filter an array to only return instances of a specific type. In the following example, we filter an array that contains instances of the `Person` protocol and have it only return those elements of the array that are instances of the `SwiftProgrammer` type:

```
for person in people where person is SwiftProgrammer {
    print("(person.firstName) is a Swift Programmer")
}
```

Now, let's look at how we would cast an instance to a specific type. To do this, we can use the `as` keyword. Since the cast can fail if the instance is not of the specified type, the `as` keyword comes in two forms: `as?` and `as!`. With the `as?` form, if the casting fails, it returns a nil. With the `as!` form, if the casting fails, a runtime error is thrown; therefore, it is recommended to use the `as?` form unless we are absolutely sure of the instance type or if we perform a check of the instance type prior to doing the cast. The following example shows how we would use the `as?` keyword to attempt to cast an instance of a variable to the `SwiftProgammer` type:

```
if let _ = person as? SwiftProgrammer {
    print("(person.firstName) is a Swift Programmer")
}
```

Since the `as?` keyword returns an optional, we could use optional binding to perform the cast.

Now, let's see how we can use associated types with protocols.

Associated types with protocols

When defining a protocol, there are times when it is useful to define one or more associated types. An associated type gives us a placeholder name that we can use within the protocol in place of a type. The actual type to use for the associated type is not defined until the protocol is adopted. The associated type basically says: *we don't know the exact type to use; therefore, when a type adopts this protocol, it will define it*. As an example, if we were to define a protocol for a queue, we would want the type that adopts the protocol to define the instance types that the queue contains rather than the protocol.

To define an associated type, we use the `associatedtype` keyword. Let's see how we can use associated types within a protocol. In this example, we will illustrate the `Queue` protocol, which will define the requirements that are needed to implement a queue:

```
protocol Queue  {
    associatedtype QueueType
    mutating func addItem(item: QueueType)
    mutating func getItem() -> QueueType?
    func count() -> Int
}
```

In this protocol, we define one associated type named `QueueType`. We then use this associated type twice within the protocol. First, we use it as the parameter type for the `addItem()` method, and then we use it again when we define the return type of the `getItem()` method as an optional type.

Any type that implements the `Queue` protocol must specify the type to use for the `QueueType` placeholder, and must also ensure that only items of that type are used where the protocol requires the `QueueType` placeholder.

Let's look at how to implement `Queue` in a non-generic class called `IntQueue`. This class will implement the `Queue` protocol using the integer type:

```
struct IntQueue: Queue  {
    var items = [Int]()
    mutating func addItem(item: Int) {
        items.append(item)
    }
    mutating func getItem() -> Int?  {
        if items.count > 0 {
            return items.remove(at:  0)
        }
        else {
            return  nil
        }
```

```
    }
    func count() -> Int {
        return items.count
    }
}
```

As we can see in the `IntQueue` structure, we use the integer type for both the parameter type of the `addItem()` method and the return type of the `getItem()` method. In this example, we implemented the `Queue` protocol in a non-generic way. Generics in Swift allow us to define the type to use at runtime rather than compile time. We will show you how to use associated types with generics in `Chapter 4`, *Generics*.

Now that we have explored protocols in some detail, let's look at how we can use them in the real world. In the next section, we will look at how to use protocols to implement the delegation design pattern.

Delegation

Delegation is used extensively within the Cocoa and Cocoa Touch frameworks. The delegation pattern is a very simple but powerful pattern where an instance of one type acts on behalf of another instance. The instance that is doing the delegating keeps a reference to the delegate instance, and then, when an action happens, the delegating instance calls the delegate to perform the intended function. Sounds confusing? It really isn't.

This design pattern is implemented in Swift by creating a protocol that defines the delegates' responsibilities. The type that conforms to the protocol, known as the delegate, will adopt this protocol, guaranteeing that it will provide the functionality that's defined by the protocol.

For the example in this section, we will have a structure named `Person`. This structure will contain two properties of the String type, named `firstName` and `lastName`. It will also have a third property that will store the delegate instance. When either the `firstName` or `lastName` properties are set, we will call a method in the delegate instance that will display the full name. Since the `Person` structure is delegating the responsibility for displaying the name to another instance, it doesn't need to know or care how the name is being displayed. Therefore, the full name could be displayed in a console window or in a UILabel; alternatively, the message may be ignored altogether.

Let's start off by looking at the protocol that defines the delegate's responsibilities. We will name this delegate `DisplayNameDelegate`:

```
protocol DisplayNameDelegate {
    func displayName(name: String)
}
```

In the `DisplayNameDelegate` protocol, we define one method that the delegate needs to implement named `displayName()`. It is assumed that, within this method, the delegate will somehow display the name; however, it is not required. The only requirement is that the delegate implements this method.

Now, let's look at the `Person` structure that uses the delegate:

```
struct Person  {
    var displayNameDelegate: DisplayNameDelegate

    var firstName = "" {
        didSet {
            displayNameDelegate.displayName(name: getFullName())
        }
    }
    var lastName =  "" {
        didSet {
            displayNameDelegate.displayName(name: getFullName())
        }
    }

    init(displayNameDelegate: DisplayNameDelegate) {
        self.displayNameDelegate = displayNameDelegate
    }

    func getFullName() -> String {
        return "\(firstName) \(lastName)"
    }
}
```

In the `Person` structure, we start off by adding the three properties, that is, `displayNameDelegate`, `firstName`, and `lastName`. The `displayNameDelegate` property contains an instance of the delegate type. This instance will be responsible for displaying the full name when the values of the `firstName` and `lastName` properties change.

Within the definitions for the `firstName` and `lastName` properties, we define the property observers. The property observers are called each time the value of the properties are changed. Within these property observers is where we call the `displayName()` method of our delegate instance to display the full name.

Now, let's create a type that will conform to the `DisplayNameDelegate` protocol. We will name this type `MyDisplayNameDelegate`:

```
struct MyDisplayNameDelegate: DisplayNameDelegate {
    func displayName(name: String)   {
        print("Name: \(name)")
    }
}
```

In this example, all we will do is print the name to the console. Now, let's see how we would use this delegate:

```
var displayDelegate = MyDisplayNameDelegate()
var person = Person(displayNameDelegate: displayDelegate)
person.firstName = "Jon"
person.lastName = "Hoffman"
```

In the preceding code, we begin by creating an instance of the `MyDisplayNameDelegate` type and then use that instance to create an instance of the `Person` type. Now, when we set the properties of the `Person` instance, the delegate is used to print the full name to the console.

While printing the name to the console may not seem that exciting, the real power of the delegation pattern comes when our application wants to change the behavior. Maybe we want to send the name to a web service or display it somewhere on the screen, or even ignore the change. To change this behavior, we simply need to create a new type that conforms to the `DisplayNameDelegate` protocol. We can then use this new type when we create an instance of the `Person` type.

Another advantage that we get from using the delegation pattern is loose coupling. In our example, we separated the logic part of our code from the view by using the delegate to display the name whenever the properties changed. Loose coupling promotes a separation of responsibility, where each type is responsible for very specific tasks; this makes it very easy to swap out these tasks when requirements change, because we all know that requirements change often.

So far in this chapter, we have looked at protocols from a coding point of view. Now, let's look at protocols from a design point of view.

Designing with protocols

With protocol-oriented programming, we should always begin our design with the protocols, but how should we design these protocols? In the object-oriented programming world, we have superclasses that contain all the base requirements for the subclasses. Protocol design is a little bit different.

In the protocol-oriented programming world, we use protocols instead of superclasses, and it is preferable to break the requirements into smaller, more specific protocols rather than having bigger monolithic protocols. In this section, we will look at how we can separate the requirements into smaller, very specific protocols and how to use protocol inheritance and composition. In Chapter 3, *Extensions*, we will take this a little further and show you how to add functionality to all types that conform to a protocol using protocol extensions.

For the example in this section, we will model something that I enjoy building: robots. There are many types of robots with lots of different sensors, so our model will need the ability to grow and handle all the different options. Since all robots have some form of movement, we will start off by creating a protocol that will define the requirements for this movement. We will name this protocol RobotMovement:

```
protocol RobotMovement {
    func forward(speedPercent: Double)
    func reverse(speedPercent: Double)
    func left(speedPercent: Double)
    func right(speedPercent: Double)
    func stop()
}
```

In this protocol, we define the five methods that all conforming types must implement. These methods will move the robot in the forward, reverse, left, or right directions, as well as stop the robot. This protocol will meet our needs if we only want the robot to travel in two dimensions, but what if we had a flying robot? For this, we would need our robot to also go up and down. To do this, we can use protocol inheritance to create a protocol that adds the additional requirements for traveling in three dimensions:

```
protocol RobotMovementThreeDimensions: RobotMovement {
    func up(speedPercent: Double)
    func down(speedPercent: Double)
}
```

Notice that we use protocol inheritance when we create this protocol to inherit the requirements from the original RobotMovement protocol. This allows us to use polymorphism, as described in the *Polymorphism with protocols* section of this chapter. This allows us to use instances of types that conform to either of these protocols interchangeably by using the interface provided by the RobotMovement protocol. We can then determine whether the robot can travel in three dimensions by using the is keyword, as described in the *Type casting with protocols* section of this chapter, to see if the RobotMovement instance conforms to the RobotMovementThreeDimensions protocol or not. Now, we need to add some sensors to our design. We will start off by creating a Sensor protocol that all other sensor types will inherit from. This protocol will contain four requirements. The first two will be read-only properties that define the name and type for the sensor. We will need an initiator that lets us name the sensor and a method that will be used to poll the sensor:

```
protocol Sensor {
    var sensorType: String {get}
    var sensorName: String {get set}

    init (sensorName: String)
    func pollSensor()
}
```

The sensor type will be used to define the type of sensor and will contain a string, such as DHT22EnvironmentSensor. The sensor name will let us distinguish between multiple sensors and will contain a string, such as RearEnvironmentSensor. The pollSensor() method will be used to perform the default operation by the sensor. Generally, this method is used to read the sensor at regular intervals. Now, we will create requirements for some specific sensor types. The following example shows how to create the requirements for an environment sensor:

```
protocol EnvironmentSensor: Sensor {
    func currentTemperature() -> Double
    func currentHumidity() -> Double
}
```

This protocol inherits the requirements from the Sensor protocol and adds two additional requirements that are unique for environment sensors. The currentTemperature() method will return the last temperature reading from the sensor and the currentHumidity() method will return the last humidity reading from the sensor. The pollSensor() method from the Sensor protocol will be used to read the temperature and humidity at regular intervals. Finally, the pollSensor() method will probably run on a separate thread. Let's go ahead and create a couple more sensor types:

```
protocol RangeSensor: Sensor {
    func setRangeNotification(rangeCentimeter: Double,
```

```
        rangeNotification: () -> Void)
    func currentRange() -> Double
}

protocol DisplaySensor: Sensor {
    func displayMessage(message: String)
}

protocol WirelessSensor: Sensor {
    func setMessageReceivedNotification(messageNotification:
        (String) -> Void)
    func messageSend(message: String)
}
```

You will notice that two of these protocols (RangeSensor and WirelessSensor) define methods that set notifications (setRangeNotification and setMessageReceivedNotifications). These methods accept closures in the method parameters and will be used within the pollSensor() method to notify robot code immediately if something has happened. With the RangeSensor types, the closure will be called if the robot is within a certain distance of an object, and with WirelessSensor types, the closure will be called if a message comes in. There are two advantages that we get from a protocol-oriented design like this one. The first is that each of the protocols only contain the requirements that are needed for their particular sensor type. The second is that we are able to use protocol composition to allow a single type to conform to multiple protocols. As an example, if we had a display sensor that has Wi-Fi built in, we would create a type that conforms to both the DisplaySensor and WirelessSensor protocols. There are many other sensor types; however, this will give us a good start for our robot. Now, let's create a protocol that will define the requirements for the robot types:

```
protocol Robot {
    var name: String {get set}
    var robotMovement: RobotMovement {get set}
    var sensors: [Sensor] {get}

    init (name: String, robotMovement: RobotMovement)
    func addSensor(sensor: Sensor)
    func pollSensors()
}
```

This protocol defines three properties, one initiator, and two methods that will need to be implemented by any type that conforms with this protocol. These requirements will give us the basic functionality that's needed for the robots. It may be a bit confusing thinking about all of these protocols, especially if we are used to having only a few superclass types. It usually helps to have a basic diagram of our protocols. The following diagram shows the protocols that we just defined with the protocol hierarchy:

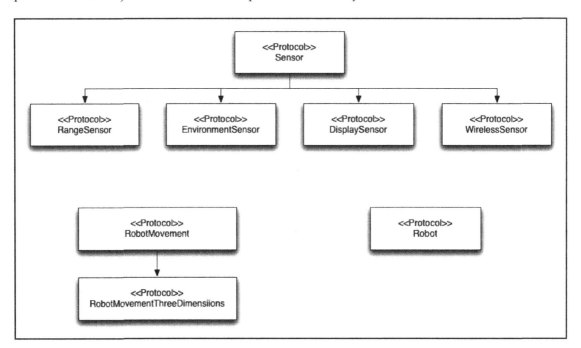

This gives us a basic idea of how to design a protocol hierarchy. You will notice that each of the protocols define the specific requirements for each device type. In Chapter 6, *Protocol-Oriented Programming,* we will go into greater detail on how to model our requirements with protocols. In this section, we used protocols to define the requirements for the components of a robot. Now it's your turn – take a moment and see if you can create a concrete implementation of the Robot protocol without creating any concrete implementations of the other protocols. The key to understanding protocols is understanding how to use them without the concrete types that conform to them. In the downloadable code for this book, we have a sample class named SixWheelRover that conforms to the Robot protocol that you can compare your implementation to. Now, let's see how Apple uses protocols in the Swift standard library.

Protocols in the Swift standard library

Apple uses protocols extensively in the Swift standard library. The best resource that we have to see the makeup of the standard library is `http://swiftdoc.org`. This site shows us the types, protocols, operators, and globals that make up the standard library. To see how Apple uses protocols, let's look at the Dictionary type. This is a very commonly used type, but also one that has a pretty simple protocol hierarchy. From the `http://swiftdoc.org/` main page, click on the Dictionary type. Then, scroll about halfway down the page until you see the Inheritance section, which should look similar to the following screenshot:

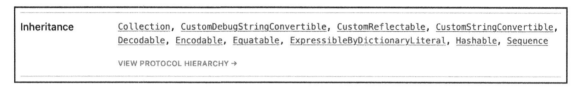

This section lists the protocols that the Dictionary type conforms to. If we click on the **View Protocol Hierarchy** → link, we will see a graphical representation of the protocol hierarchy, which will look similar to this:

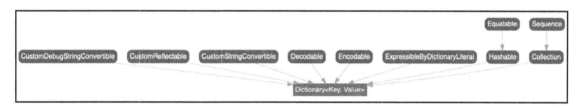

As we can see from the preceding diagram, the **Dictionary** type conforms to five different protocols. We can also see that the **Collection** protocol inherits requirements from the **Sequence** protocol.

From the `http://swiftdoc.org/` main page, we can click on each of the protocols to see their requirements. From this site, we can see that Apple uses protocols extensively within the Swift standard library. We will be looking at this site as we go through this book to see how Apple uses the various technologies that we are discussing.

Summary

While protocols themselves may not seem very exciting, they are actually quite powerful. As we saw in this chapter, we are able to use them to create very specific requirements. We can then use protocol inheritance and protocol composition to create protocol hierarchies. We also saw how to implement delegation patterns with protocols.

We concluded this chapter by showing you how we can model a robot with sensors using protocols and how Apple uses protocols in the Swift standard library.

In `Chapter 3`, *Extensions*, we will see how we can use protocol extensions to add functionality to types that conform to a protocol, but before we do that, let's look at our type choices.

2
Our Type Choices

In most traditional, object-oriented programming languages, we create classes (which are reference types) as blueprints for our objects. In Swift, unlike other object-oriented languages, structures have much of the same functionality as classes; however, they are value types. Apple has said that we should prefer value types, such as structures, to reference types, but what are the actual advantages? Swift actually has a number of type choices that we can use, and in this chapter we will look at all of these types to see their advantages and disadvantages. Knowing how and when to use each type is important in order to properly implement protocol-oriented programming in our projects.

In this chapter, you will learn the following:

- What a class is and how to use it
- What a structure is and how to use it
- What an enumeration is and how to use it
- What a tuple is and how to use it
- The differences between value and reference types

In Swift, types are classified as either named or compound types. A named type is a type that can be given a name when it is defined. These named types include classes, structures, enumerations, and protocols. In addition to user-defined named types, Swift also defines many commonly used named types within the Swift standard library, including arrays, sets, and dictionaries.

Many data types that we would normally consider primitive types in other languages are actually named types in Swift and are implemented in the Swift standard library using structures. These include types that represent numbers, strings, characters, and Boolean values. Since these types are implemented as named types, we are able to extend their behavior using extensions as we would with any other named type. As we will see in both this and future chapters, the ability to extend a named type, including types that would traditionally be considered as primitive types and protocols, is an extremely powerful feature of the Swift language and is one of the pillars of protocol-oriented programming. We will look at extensions in Chapter 3, *Extensions*.

A compound type is a type that is not given a name when it is defined. In Swift, we have two compound types: function types and tuple types. Function types represent closures, functions, and methods, while tuple types take the form of a comma-separated list that is enclosed in parentheses. We are able to use the type alias declaration to give an alias to compound types. This allows us to use the alias name instead of the type itself within our code.

There are also two categories of types: reference types and value types. When we pass an instance of a reference type, we are passing a reference to the original instance, which means that the two references are sharing the same instance. Classes are reference types.

When we pass an instance of a value type, we are passing a new copy of the instance, which means that each instance gets a unique copy. Value types include structures, enumerations, and tuples.

Every type in Swift will be either a named or compound type, and they will also be either a reference or value type, except in the case of protocols. Since we are unable to create an instance of a protocol, it is neither a reference nor a value type. Sounds a bit confusing? It really isn't. As we look at all type choices and how we use them, we will see how easy this is to understand.

Now, let's begin looking at the type choices that we have in Swift. We will begin by looking at the backbone of object-oriented programming: the class.

Classes

In object-oriented programming, we cannot create an object without a blueprint that tells the application what properties and methods to expect from the object. In most object-oriented languages, this blueprint comes in the form of a class. A class is a construct that allows us to encapsulate the properties, methods, and initializers of an object into a single type. Classes can also include other items, such as subscripts; however, we are going to focus on the basic items that make up classes, not only in Swift, but in other languages as well.

Let's look at how we would use a class in Swift:

```swift
class Myclass {
    var oneProperty: String

    init(oneProperty: String) {
        self.oneProperty = oneProperty
    }
```

```
func oneFunction() {

}
}
```

An instance of a class is typically called an object. However, in Swift, structures and classes have many of the same functionalities; therefore, we will use the term instance when referring to instances of either type.

Anyone who has used object-oriented programming in the past is probably familiar with the class type. It has been the backbone of object-oriented programming since its inception.

When we create instances of the class, it is named; therefore, the class is a named type. It is also a reference type.

The next type we are going to look at is arguably the most important type in the Swift language: structures.

Structures

Apple has said that Swift developers should prefer value types over reference types, and it seems that they have also taken that philosophy to heart. If we look at the Swift standard library (http://swiftdoc.org), we will see that the majority of types are implemented using structures. The reason Apple is able to implement the majority of Swift's standard library with structures is that, in Swift, structures have many of the same functionalities as classes. There are, however, some fundamental differences between classes and structures, and we will be looking at these differences later in this chapter.

In Swift, a structure is a construct that allows us to encapsulate the properties, methods, and initializers of an instance into a single type. They can also include other items, such as subscripts. However, we are going to focus on the basic items that make up a structure. This description may sound a lot like how we described classes in the last section. This is because classes and structures are very similar in Swift. I know we have already mentioned this, but it is very important to understand the ways in which structures and classes are similar, and it is also necessary to understand the ways in which they are different, in order to know which type to use.

Let's see how we could create a structure:

```
struct MyStruct {
    var oneProperty: String

    func oneFunction() {
    }
}
```

If we compare this structure to the class from the previous section, we can see some very basic differences. In the structure, we are not required to define an initializer because the structure will create a default initializer for us if we do not provide one to set any properties that need to be initialized. This default initializer will require us to provide initial values for all non-optional properties when we create an instance of the structure.

One difference that we do not see here is that the mutating keyword is used for some of the methods defined in the structures. Structures are value types; therefore, by default, the properties of the structure cannot be changed from within instance methods. By using the mutating keyword, we are opting for the mutating behavior for that particular method. We must use the mutating keyword for any method within the structure that changes the values of the structure's properties.

The structure is a named type because we name the instance when it is created. It is also a value type. One of the main differences between a structure and a class is that the class is a reference type while a structure is a value type. We will look at the differences between value and reference types later in this chapter.

Let's look at how access controls work for classes and structures in Swift.

Access controls

Access controls allow us to restrict the access to, and visibility of, parts of the code. This allows us to hide implementation details and only expose the interfaces we want the external code to access. We can assign specific access levels to both classes and structures. We can also assign specific access levels to properties, methods, and initializers that belong to our classes and structures.

In Swift, there are five access levels:

- **Open**: This is the most visible access control level. It allows us to use a property, method, class, and so on anywhere we want to import the module. Basically, anything can use an item that has an access control level set to open. Anything that is marked open can be subclassed or overridden by any item within the module they are defined in, and any module that imports the module it is defined in. This level is primarily used by frameworks to expose the framework's public API.
- **Public**: This access level allows us to use a property, method, class, and so on anywhere we want in order to import the module. Basically, anything can use an item that has an access control level set to public. Anything that is marked public can be subclassed or overridden by any item within the module they are defined in. This level is primarily used by frameworks to expose the framework's public API.
- **Internal**: This is the default access level. This access level allows us to use a property, method, class, and so on, in the module the item is defined in. If this level is used in a framework, it lets other parts of the framework use the item, but code outside the framework will be unable to access it.
- **Fileprivate**: This access control allows access to the properties and methods from any code within the same source file that the item is defined in.
- **Private**: This is the least visible access control level. It only allows us to use the property, method, class, and so on in the source file that defines it.

Access controls are extremely useful when we are developing frameworks. In order to use frameworks, we need to mark the public-facing interfaces as public, so that other modules, such as the applications that import the framework, can use them. We would then use the internal and private access control levels to mark the interfaces that we want to use internal framework.

To define access levels, we place the name of the level before the definition of the entity. The following code shows examples of how we would add access levels to several entities:

```
private struct EmployeeStruct {}
public var firstName = "Jon"
internal var lastName = "Hoffman"
private var salaryYear = 0.0
public func getFullName() -> String {}
fileprivate func giveBonus(amount: Double) {}
open func giveRaise(amount: Double) {}
```

There are some limitations with access controls, but these limitations are there to ensure that access levels in Swift follow a simple guiding principle: *no entity can be defined in terms of another entity that has a lower (more restrictive) access level*. What this means is that we cannot assign a higher (less restrictive) access level to an entity when it relies on another entity that has a lower (more restrictive) access level.

Here are a couple of examples to illustrate this rule:

- We cannot mark a method as being public when one of the arguments or the return type has an access level set to private because the external code would not have access to the private type.
- We cannot set the access level of a method or property to public when the class or structure has an access level set to private because the external code would not be able to access the constructor when the class is private.

The next type that we are going to look at is Swift's supercharged enumerations.

Enumerations

In most languages, enumerations are little more than a data type consisting of a set of named values called elements. In Swift, however, enumerations have been supercharged to give them significantly more power. Enumerations in Swift are a lot closer in functionality to classes and structures; however, they can still be used like enumerations in other languages.

Before we see how enumerations are supercharged in Swift, let's see how we can use them as standard enumerations. The following code defines the `Devices` enumeration:

```
enum Devices {
    case iPod
    case iPhone
    case iPad
}
```

In the `Devices` enumeration, we defined three possible values: `iPod`, `iPhone`, and `iPad`. One of the reasons why enumerations are different in Swift, as compared to other languages, is that they can be prepopulated with values known as raw values. As shown in the following code example, we could redefine our `Devices` enumeration to be prepopulated with `String` values:

```
enum Devices: String {
    case iPod = "iPod"
    case iPhone = "iPhone"
```

```
    case iPad = "iPad"
}
```

We can then use the `rawValue` property to retrieve the raw value for any of the enumeration's elements, as shown in the following code:

```
Devices.iPod.rawValue
```

In Swift, we can also store the associated values alongside our case values. These associated values can be of any type, and can vary for each case. This enables us to store additional custom information with our case types. Let's see how this works by redefining our `Devices` enumeration with the associated values:

```
enum Devices {
    case iPod(model: Int, year: Int, memory: Int)
    case iPhone(model: String, memory: Int)
    case iPad(model: String, memory: Int)
}
```

In the previous example, we defined three associated values with the iPod case and two associated values with the iPhone and iPad cases. We can then use this new `Devices` enumeration with the associated values, as follows:

```
var myPhone = Devices.iPhone(model: "6", memory: 64)
var myTablet = Devices.iPad(model: "Pro", memory: 128)
```

In the previous example, we defined the `myPhone` device as an iPhone 6 with 64 GB of memory and the `myTablet` device as an iPod Pro with 128 GB of memory. We can now retrieve the associated values as follows:

```
switch myPhone  {
    case .iPod(let model, let year, let memory):
      print("iPod: \(model) \(memory)")
    case .iPhone(let  model,  let  memory):
      print("iPhone: \(model) \(memory)")
    case .iPad(let model, let  memory):
      print("iPad: \(model) \(memory)")
}
```

In this example, we will simply print out the associated values of the `myPhone` device. What we have seen so far makes enumerations far more powerful than enumerations in other languages. However, we are not done demonstrating what enumerations can do in Swift. In Swift, enumerations are not limited to a list of elements. They can also contain computed properties, initializers, and methods, just like classes and structures.

Let's take a look at how we can use methods and computed properties with enumerations. Since it almost feels like Christmas with all the exciting features, our example will have a holiday theme:

```
enum Reindeer: String {
    case dasher, dancer, prancer, vixen, comet, cupid, donner, blitzen,
        rudolph
    static var allCases: [Reindeer] {
        return [dasher, dancer, prancer, vixen, comet, cupid, donner,
            blitzen, rudolph]
    }
    static func randomCase() -> Reindeer {
        let randomValue = Int(
            arc4random_uniform(
                UInt32(allCases.count)
            )
        )
        return allCases[randomValue]
    }
}
```

In this example, we created the `Reindeer` enumeration that contains the names of Santa's nine reindeer (we cannot forget Rudolph, you know). Within the `Reindeer` enumeration, we created an `allCases` computed property that returns an array containing all the possible cases for the enumeration. We also created a `randomCase()` method that will return a random reindeer from our enumeration.

The previous examples in this section showed how to use the individual features of Swift's enumerations, but their true power is shown when they are used together. Let's look at one more example in which we combine the associated values with methods and properties to make a supercharged enumeration. We will start off by defining a basic enumeration that defines the various formats of a book, with the page count and the price of each format stored in an associated value:

```
enum BookFormat {
    case paperBack (pageCount: Int, price: Double)
    case hardCover (pageCount: Int, price: Double)
    case pdf (pageCount: Int, price: Double)
    case ePub (pageCount: Int, price: Double)
    case kindle (pageCount: Int, price: Double)
}
```

This enumeration would work great, but there are some basic drawbacks. The first one, and the one that really drives me nuts, is seen when we retrieve the associated values from our enumerations. For example, let's create the following instance of the `BookFormat` enumeration:

```
var paperBack = BookFormat.paperBack(pageCount: 220, price: 39.99)
```

Now, to retrieve the page count and the price of this enumeration, we could use the following code:

```
switch paperBack {
    case .paperBack(let pageCount,  let price):
       print("\(pageCount) - \(price)")
    case .hardCover(let pageCount,  let price):
       print("\(pageCount) - \(price)")
    case .pdf(let  pageCount,  let price):
       print("\(pageCount) - \(price)")
    case .ePub(let  pageCount,  let price):
       print("\(pageCount) - \(price)")
    case .kindle(let  pageCount,  let price):
       print("\(pageCount) - \(price)")
}
```

This is quite a bit of code to retrieve the associated values, especially where we may need to retrieve these values in multiple locations throughout our code. We could create a global function that would retrieve these values, but we have a better way in Swift. We can add a computed property to our enumeration that will retrieve `pageCount` and the price values of the enumeration.

The following example shows how we could add these computed properties:

```
enum BookFormat {
    case paperBack (pageCount: Int, price: Double)
    case hardCover (pageCount: Int, price: Double)
    case pdf (pageCount: Int, price: Double)
    case ePub (pageCount: Int, price: Double)
    case kindle (pageCount: Int, price: Double)

    var pageCount: Int {
        switch self {
            case .paperBack(let pageCount, _):
                return pageCount
            case .hardCover(let  pageCount, _):
                return pageCount
            case .pdf(let pageCount, _):
                return pageCount
            case .ePub(let  pageCount, _):
```

```
                            return pageCount
                    case .kindle(let  pageCount, _):
                        return pageCount
            }
        }
        var price: Double {
            switch self {
                case .paperBack(_, let price):
                    return  price
                case .hardCover(_, let price):
                    return  price
                case .pdf(_,  let price):
                    return  price
                case .ePub(_, let price):
                    return  price
                case .kindle(_, let price):
                    return price
            }
        }
    }
```

With these computed properties, we can retrieve the associated values from the `BookFormat` enumeration very easily. The following code demonstrates how to use them:

```
var paperBack = BookFormat.paperBack(pageCount: 220, price: 39.99)
print("\(paperBack.pageCount) - \(paperBack.price)")
```

These computed properties hide the complexity of the `switch` statement and provide a much cleaner dot syntax interface to use. It also encapsulates the code to retrieve the associated property within the enumeration, rather than having it embedded throughout our code.

We can also add methods to our enumerations. Let's say, as an example, that, if a person were to buy multiple copies of our book in different formats, they would receive a 20% discount. The following function could be added to our `BookFormat` enumeration in order to calculate this discount:

```
func purchaseTogether(otherFormat: BookFormat) -> Double {
    return (self.price + otherFormat.price) * 0.80
}
```

We could now use the method as shown in the following code:

```
var paperBack = BookFormat.paperBack(pageCount: 220, price: 39.99)
var pdf = BookFormat.pdf(pageCount: 180, price: 14.99)
var total = paperBack.purchaseTogether(otherFormat: pdf)
```

As we can see, enumerations in Swift are a lot more powerful than enumerations in most other languages. The one thing to avoid is overusing them. They are not meant to be a replacement for either the class or the structure. Deep down, enumerations are still a data type consisting of a finite set of named values, and all of these new exciting features are there to make them more useful to us.

In all of the previous sample code, we had a case statement that handled each value of the enumeration with a case statement in the switch statement. This meant that we did not need to use the default case within the switch statement. If we did not have a case statement for each value of the enumeration, we could add a default case. It is recommended that we use the `@unknown` attribute with the default case so we will receive a warning if there is a value that is not handled. The following example shows us how to add the default case with the `@unknown` attribute:

```swift
enum BookFormat {
    case paperBack (pageCount: Int, price: Double)
    case hardCover (pageCount: Int, price: Double)
    case pdf (pageCount: Int, price: Double)
    case ePub (pageCount: Int, price: Double)
    case kindle (pageCount: Int, price: Double)
    var pageCount: Int {
        switch self {
        case .paperBack(let pageCount, _):
            return pageCount
        case .hardCover(let pageCount, _):
            return pageCount
        case .pdf(let pageCount, _):
            return pageCount
        case .ePub(let pageCount, _):
            return pageCount
        case .kindle(let pageCount, _):
            return pageCount
        @unknown default:
            return 0
        }
    }
    var price: Double {
        switch self {
        case .paperBack(_, let price):
            return price
        case .hardCover(_, let price):
            return price
        case .pdf(_, let price):
            return price
        case .ePub(_, let price):
            return price
```

```
        case .kindle(_, let price):
            return price
        @unknown default:
            return 0
        }
    }
}
```

When we create instances of the enumeration, it is named; therefore, it is a named type. The enumeration type is also a value type. Now, let's look at one of the most underutilized types in Swift: tuples.

Tuples

In Swift, a tuple is a finite, ordered, comma-separated list of elements. While there are tuples in other languages that I have used, I never really took advantage of them. To be honest, I was only vaguely aware that they actually existed in those other languages. In Swift, tuples are more prominent than they are in other languages, which forced me to take a closer look at them. What I found is that they are extremely useful.

 In my opinion, tuples are one of the most underutilized types in Swift and, as we go through this book (especially in the case study section), I will point out some cases where the tuple type can be used.

We can create a tuple and access the information within it as follows:

```
let mathGrade1 = ("Jon", 100)
let (name, score) = mathGrade1
print("\(name) - \(score)")
```

In the previous code, we grouped a String and an Integer into a single tuple type. We then decomposed the tuple using pattern matching, which places the values into the name and score constants.

What we saw in the previous example is an unnamed tuple. These tuples work great at a pinch, but I have found that I use named tuples more often because it is much easier to retrieve the values from a named tuple. We can create a named tuple and access the information stored within it as follows:

```
let mathGrade2 = (name: "Jon", grade: 100)
print("\(mathGrade2.name) - \(mathGrade2.grade)")
```

Note that, when we grouped the String and Integer values in this tuple, we assigned names to each of the values. We can then use these names to access the information within the tuple, thereby avoiding the decomposing step.

Apple has stated that we can use tuples as a return type for a function to return multiple values. The following example shows how we could use tuples to return multiple values from a function:

```
func calculateTip(billAmount: Double,tipPercent: Double) -> (tipAmount:
Double, totalAmount:  Double) {
    let tip = billAmount * (tipPercent/100)
    let total = billAmount + tip
    return (tipAmount:  tip, totalAmount: total)
}
```

In this example, we created a `calculateTip()` function that calculates the tip based on the `billAmount` and `tipPercentage` parameters that were passed in. Then, we returned both the tip amount that was calculated, as well as the total bill amount in a named tuple value.

We could then use this function as follows:

```
var tip = calculateTip(billAmount:31.98, tipPercent: 20)
print("\(tip.tipAmount) - \(tip.totalAmount)")
```

In this section, we have seen how tuples are typically used in Swift. As we go through this book, we will be using tuples in various examples. Tuples are very useful when we need to pass a temporary collection of values in our code.

In Swift, a tuple is a value type. Tuples are also compound types; however, we are able to give a tuple an alias using the `typealias` keyword. The following example shows how we would assign an alias to a tuple:

```
 typealias myTuple = (tipAmount: Double, totalAmount: Double)
```

In Swift, protocols are also considered a type.

Protocols

To some, it may seem surprising that protocols are considered a type, since we cannot actually create an instance of them; however, we can use them as a type. What this statement means is that, when we define the type for a variable, constant, tuple, or collection, we can use a protocol for that type.

We are not going to cover protocols in depth in this section since we have already covered them in Chapter 1, *Starting with the Protocol*; however, it is important to understand that they are considered a type.

Each type that we have discussed so far is either a value or a reference type; however, a protocol is neither, because we are not able to create an instance of them.

It is really important to have a complete understanding of the differences between value and reference types in Swift, so let's compare the two.

Value and reference types

There are some fundamental differences between value types (structures, enumerations, and tuples) and reference types (classes). The primary difference is how the instances of value and reference types are passed. When we pass an instance of a value type, we are actually passing a copy of the original instance. This means that the changes made to one instance are not reflected back to the others. When we pass an instance of a reference type, we are passing a reference to the original instance. This means that both references point to the same instance; therefore, a change made to one reference will reflect in the others.

The explanation in the previous paragraph is a pretty straightforward explanation; however, it is a very important concept that you must understand. In this section, we are going to examine the differences between value and reference types, so that we know the advantages of each, as well as the pitfalls to avoid when using them.

Let's begin by creating two types. One is going to be a structure (value type) and the other is going to be a class (reference type). We will be using these types in this section to demonstrate the differences between value and reference types. The first type that we will look at will be named MyValueType. We will implement MyValueType using a structure, which means that it is a value type, as its name tells us:

```
struct MyValueType {
    var name: String
    var assignment: String
    var grade: Int
}
```

Within `MyValueType`, we defined three properties. Two of the properties are of the String type (`name` and `assignment`), and one is of the Integer type (`grade`). Now, let's look at how we would implement this as a class:

```
class MyReferenceType {
    var name: String
    var assignment: String
    var grade: Int

    init(name: String, assignment: String, grade: Int) {
        self.name = name
        self.assignment = assignment
        self.grade = grade
    }
}
```

The `MyReferenceType` type defines the same three properties as the `MyValueType` type; however, we needed to define an initializer in the `MyReferenceType` type that we did not need to define in the `MyValueType` type. The reason for this, is that structures provide us with a default initializer that will initialize all the properties that need to be initialized if we do not provide a default initializer.

Let's look at how we could use each of these types. The following code shows how we could create instances of each of these types:

```
var ref = MyReferenceType(name: "Jon", assignment: "Math Test 1",
                          grade: 90)
var val = MyValueType(name: "Jon", assignment: "Math Test 1",
                      grade: 90)
```

As we see in this code, instances of structures are created in exactly the same way as the instances of classes. Being able to use the same format to create instances of structures and classes is good because it makes our lives easier; however, we do need to keep in mind that value types behave in a different manner to reference types. Let's look at this. The first thing we need to do is create two functions that will change the grades for the instances of the two types:

```
func extraCreditReferenceType(ref: MyReferenceType, extraCredit: Int) {
    ref.grade += extraCredit
}

func extraCreditValueType(val: MyValueType, extraCredit: Int) {
    var val = val
    val.grade += extraCredit
}
```

Each of these functions takes an instance of one of our types and an extra credit amount. Within the function, we will add the extra credit amount to the grade. Now, let's see what happens when we use each of these functions. Let's start off by seeing what happens when we use the `MyReferenceType` type with the `extraCreditReferenceType()` function:

```
var ref = MyReferenceType(name: "Jon", assignment: "Math Test 1",
                          grade: 90)
extraCreditReferenceType(ref: ref, extraCredit: 5)
print("Reference: \(ref.name) - \(ref.grade)")
```

In this code, we created an instance of the `MyReferenceType` type with a grade of 90. We then used the `extraCreditReferenceType()` function to add five extra points to the grade. If we run this code, the following line will be printed in the console:

```
Reference: Jon - 95
```

As we can see, five extra credit points were added to the grade. Now, let's try to do the same thing with the `MyValueType` type and the `extraCreditValueType()` function. The following code shows us how to do this:

```
var val = MyValueType(name: "Jon", assignment: "Math Test  1", grade: 90)
extraCreditValueType(val: val, extraCredit: 5)
print("Value: \(val.name) - \(val.grade)")
```

In this code, we created an instance of the `MyValueType` type with a grade of 90. We then used the `extraCreditValueType()` function to add five extra points to the grade. If we run this code, the following line will be printed in the console:

```
Value: Jon - 90
```

As we can see, the five extra credit points are missing from our grade in this example. The reason for this is that, when we pass an instance of a value type to a function, we are actually passing a copy of the original instance. This means that, when we add the extra credit to the grade within the `extraCreditValueType()` function, we are adding it to a copy of the original instance. As a result, the changes are not reflected back to the original copy of the instance.

Using a value type protects us from making accidental changes to our instances because the instances are scoped to the function or type in which they are created. Value types also protect us from having multiple references to the same instance. Let's look at this so we can understand the types of issues we may face when we use reference types. We will begin by creating a function that is designed to retrieve the grade for an assignment from a data store. However, to simplify our example, we will simply generate a random score. The following code shows us how we would write this function:

```
func getGradeForAssignment(assignment: MyReferenceType)  {
    // Code to get grade from DB
    // Random code here to illustrate issue
    let num = Int(arc4random_uniform(20) + 80)
    assignment.grade = num
    print("Grade  for \(assignment.name) is \(num)")
}
```

This function is designed to retrieve the grade for the assignment that is defined in the `MyReferenceType` instance that is passed into the function. Once the grade is retrieved, we will use it to set the grade property of the `MyReferenceType` instance. We will also print the grade out to the console so we can see what the grade is. Now, let's see how we would not want to use this function:

```
var mathGrades = [MyReferenceType]()
var students = ["Jon", "Kim", "Kailey", "Kara"]
var mathAssignment = MyReferenceType(name: "", assignment:
"MathAssignment", grade: 0)

for student in students  {
    mathAssignment.name = student
    getGradeForAssignment(assignment: mathAssignment)
    mathGrades.append(mathAssignment)
}
```

In the previous code, we created a `mathGrades` array that will store the grades for our assignment, and a `students` array that will contain the names of the students whom we wish to retrieve the grades for. We then created an instance of the `MyReferenceType` class that contains the name of our assignment. We will use this instance to request the grades from the `getGradeForAssignment()` function. Now that everything is defined, we will loop through the list of students in order to retrieve the grades. The following is a sample output from this code:

```
Grade for Jon is 90
Grade for Kim is 84
Grade for Kailey is 99
Grade for Kara is 89
```

This appears to look exactly how we want it to. However, there is a huge bug in this code. Let's loop through our `mathGrades` array to see what grades we have in the array itself:

```
for assignment in mathGrades {
    print("\(assignment.name): grade \(assignment.grade)")
}
```

The output of this code would look as follows:

```
Kara: grade 89
Kara: grade 89
Kara: grade 89
Kara: grade 89
```

That is not what we wanted. The reason why we are seeing these results is because we created one instance of the `MyReferenceType` type, and then we kept updating that single instance. This means that we kept overwriting the previous name and grade. Since `MyReferenceType` is a reference type, all the references in the `mathGrades` array pointed to the same instance of the `MyReferenceType` type, which ended up being Kara's grade. Most experienced object-oriented developers have learned to watch out for these types of issues the hard way, but this type of error still happens, especially with junior developers. Using value types can help us avoid these issues; however, there are times when we would like to have this type of behavior. Apple has provided a way for us to have this behavior with value types using `inout` parameters. An `inout` parameter allows us to change the value of a value type parameter and to have that change persist after the function call has ended.

We define an `inout` parameter by placing the `inout` keyword at the start of the parameter's definition. An `inout` parameter has a value that is passed into the function. This value is then modified by the function and is passed back out of the function to replace the original value. Let's look at how we can use value types with the `inout` keyword to create a version of the previous example that will work correctly. The first thing we need to do is modify the `getGradesForAssignment()` function to use an instance of `MyValueType` that it can modify:

```
func getGradeForAssignment(assignment: inout MyValueType) {
    // Code  to  get grade from DB
    // Random  code here to illustrate issue
    let num = Int(arc4random_uniform(20) + 80)
    assignment.grade = num
    print("Grade for \(assignment.name)  is \(num)")
}
```

The only change we made to this function was the way we defined the parameter that was passed in. The property is now defined as being of the `MyValueType` type, and we added the `inout` keyword to allow the function to modify the instance that was passed in. Now let's see how we could use this function:

```
var mathGrades = [MyValueType]()
var students  = ["Jon", "Kim", "Kailey", "Kara"]
var mathAssignment = MyValueType(name: "", assignment: "Math Assignment",
                                 grade: 0)
for student in students  {
    mathAssignment.name = student
    getGradeForAssignment(assignment: &mathAssignment)
    mathGrades.append(mathAssignment)
}

for assignment in mathGrades {
    print("\(assignment.name): grade \(assignment.grade)")
}
```

Once again, this code looks a lot like the code from the previous example; however, we made two changes. The first is that the `mathAssignment` variable is now defined to be of the `MyValueType` type and, when we called the `getGradeForAssignment()` function, we prefixed the argument with an ampersand (&). The ampersand tells us that we are passing a reference to the value type, so any changes made in the function are reflected back to the original instance.

The output of this new code will look as follows:

```
Grade for Jon is 87
Grade for Kim is 81
Grade for Kailey is 90
Grade for Kara is 83
Jon: grade 87
Kim: grade 81
Kailey: grade 90
Kara: grade 83
```

The output from this code is what we expected to see, where each instance in the `mathGrades` array represents a different grade. The reason this code works correctly is that when we add the `mathAssignment` instance to the `mathGrades` array, we are adding a copy of the `mathAssignment` instance to the array. However, when we pass the `mathAssignment` instance to the `getGradeForAssignment()` function, we are passing a reference, even though the type is a value type.

There are some things we cannot do with value types that we can do with reference (class) types. The first thing that we will look at is the recursive data type.

Recursive data types for reference types only

A recursive data type is a type that contains other values of the same type as a property for the type. Recursive data types are used when we want to define dynamic data structures such as lists and trees. The size of these dynamic data structures can grow or shrink, depending on our runtime requirements.

Linked lists are perfect examples of a dynamic data structure that we would implement using a recursive data type. A linked list is a group of nodes that are linked together and where, in its simplest form, each node maintains a link to the next node in the list. The following diagram shows how a very basic linked list works:

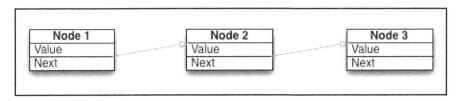

Each node in the list contains some value or data, and it also contains the link to the next node in the list. If one of the nodes within the list loses the reference to the next node, the remainder of the list will be lost because each node is only aware of the next node. Some linked lists maintain a link to both the previous and next nodes, in order to allow us to move both forward and backward through the list.

The following code shows how we could create a linked list using a reference type:

```
class LinkedListReferenceType {
    var value: String
    var next: LinkedListReferenceType?
    init(value: String) {
        self.value = value
    }
}
```

In the `LinkedListReferenceType` class, we have two properties. The first property is named `value` and it contains the data for this instance. The second property is named `next` and it points to the next item in the linked list. If the next property is `nil`, then this instance will be the last node in the list. If we tried to implement this linked list as a value type, the code could look similar to the following code:

```
struct LinkedListValueType  {
    var value: String
    var next: LinkedListValueType?
}
```

When we add this code to a playground, we receive the following error: **Recursive value type 'LinkedListValueType' is not allowed**. This tells us that Swift does not allow recursive value types. However, we are able to implement them as a reference type, which we saw earlier. If we think about it, recursive value types are a really bad idea because of how value types function. Let's examine this for a minute, because it will really stress the difference between value and reference types. It will also help you understand why we need reference types. Let's say that we were able to create the `LinkedListValueType` structure without any errors. Now let's create three nodes for our list, as shown in the following code:

```
var one = LinkedListValueType(value: "One",next: nil)
var two = LinkedListValueType  (value: "Two",next: nil)
var three = LinkedListValueType  (value: "Three",next: nil)
```

Now we will link these nodes together with the following code:

```
one.next  =  two
two.next = three
```

Do you see the problem with this code? If not, think about how a value type is passed. In the first line, `one.next=two`, we are not actually setting the `next` property to the `two` instance itself, we are setting it to a copy of the `two` instance. This means that in the next line, `two.next=three`, we are setting the next property of the `two` instance to the `three` instance. However, this change is not reflected back in the copy that was made for the `next` property of the `one` instance. Does this sound a little confusing?

Let's clear it up a little by looking at a diagram that shows the state of our three `LinkedListValueType` instances if we were able to run this code:

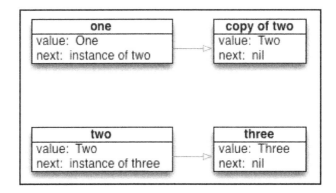

As we can see from the diagram, the `next` property of the `one` instance is pointing to a copy of the `two` instance, whose `next` property is still nil. The `next` property of the original `two` instance, however, is pointing to the `three` instance. This means that, if we try to go through the list by starting at the `one` instance, we will not reach the `three` instance because the copy of the `two` instance will still have a `next` property that is nil.

The second thing that we can only do with reference (class) types is class inheritance.

Inheritance for reference types only

In object-oriented programming, inheritance refers to one class (known as a sub or child class) being derived from another class (known as a super or parent class). The subclass will inherit methods, properties, and other characteristics from the superclass. With inheritance, we can also create a class hierarchy where we can have multiple layers of inheritance.

Let's look at how we could create a class hierarchy with classes in Swift. We will start off by creating a base class named `Animal`:

```
class Animal {
    var numberOfLegs = 0
    func sleeps() {
        print("zzzzz")
    }
    func walking() {
        print("Walking  on \(numberOfLegs) legs")
    }
```

```
    func speaking() {
        print("No sound")
    }
}
```

In the `Animal` class, we defined one property (`numberOfLegs`) and three methods (`sleeps()`, `walking()`, and `speaking()`). Now, any class that is a subclass of the `Animal` class will also have these properties and methods. Let's see how this works by creating two classes that are subclasses of the `Animal` class. These two classes will be named `Biped` (an animal with two legs) and `Quadruped` (an animal with four legs):

```
class Biped: Animal {
    override init() {
        super.init()
        numberOfLegs = 2
    }
}

class Quadruped: Animal {
    override init() {
        super.init()
        numberOfLegs = 4
    }
}
```

Since these two classes inherit all the properties and methods from the `Animal` class, all we need to do is create an initializer that sets the `numberOfLegs` property to the correct number of legs. Now, let's add another layer of inheritance by creating a `Dog` class that will be a subclass of the `Quadruped` class:

```
class Dog: Quadruped {
    override func speaking() {
        print("Barking")
    }
}
```

In the `Dog` class, we inherited from the `Quadruped` class that inherits from the `Animal` class. Therefore, the `Dog` class will have all the properties, methods, and characteristics of both the `Animal` and `Quadruped` classes. If the `Quadruped` class overrides anything from the `Animal` class, then the `Dog` class will inherit the version from the `Quadruped` class. We can create very complex class hierarchies in this manner. As an example, the following diagram expands on the class hierarchy that we just created to add several other animal classes:

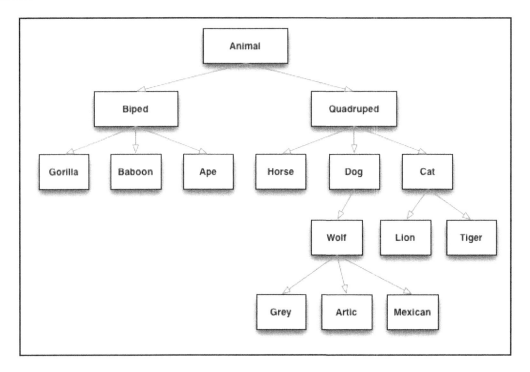

As we can see, class hierarchies can get very complex. However, as we just saw, they can eliminate a lot of duplicate code because our subclasses inherit methods, properties, and other characteristics from their superclasses. Therefore, we do not need to recreate them in all of the subclasses.

The biggest drawback of a class hierarchy is the complexity. When we have a complex hierarchy, as shown in the preceding diagram, it is easy to make a change and not realize how it is going to affect all of the subclasses. As an example, if we think about the dog and cat classes, we may want to add a `furColor` property to our `Quadruped` class so we can set the color of the animal's fur. However, horses do not have fur; they have hair. So, before we can make any changes to a class in our hierarchy, we need to understand how it will affect all the subclasses in the hierarchy.

In Swift, it is best to avoid using complex class hierarchies, as shown in this example, and use a protocol-oriented approach, unless there are specific reasons to use them. We will see how to use a protocol-oriented approach to avoid complex class hierarchies throughout this book.

In most object-oriented languages, the standard library is in the form of a class hierarchy, where the majority of the library is implemented using classes, as shown in this section. However, Swift is a bit different.

Dynamic dispatch

In the *Inheritance for reference types only* section, we saw how we can use inheritance with classes to inherit and override functionality defined in a superclass. You may be wondering how and when the appropriate implementation is chosen. The process of choosing which implementation to call is performed at runtime and is known as dynamic dispatch.

One of the key points to understand from the previous paragraph is that the implementation is chosen at runtime. What that means is that a certain amount of runtime overhead is associated with using class inheritance, as shown in the *Inheritance for reference types only* section. For most applications, this overhead is not a concern; however, for performance-sensitive applications such as games, this overhead can be costly.

One of the ways that we can reduce the overhead associated with dynamic dispatch is to use the `final` keyword. The `final` keyword puts a restriction on the class, method, or function that indicates that it cannot be overridden, in the case of a method or function, or subclassed, in the case of a class.

To use the `final` keyword, you put it prior to the class, method, or function declaration, as shown in the following example:

```
final func myFunc() {}
final var myProperty = 0
final class MyClass {}
```

In the *Inheritance for reference types only* section, we defined a class hierarchy that started with the `Animal` superclass. If we wanted to restrict subclasses from overriding the `walking()` method and `numberOfLegs` property, we would change the `Animal` implementation, as shown in the following example:

```
class Animal {
    final var numberOfLegs = 0
    func sleeps() {
        print("zzzzz")
```

```
    }
    final func walking() {
        print("Walking on \(numberOfLegs) legs")
    }
    func speaking() {
        print("No sound")
    }
}
```

This change allows the application, at runtime, to make a direct call to the `walking()` method rather than an indirect call that gives the application a slight performance increase. If you must use a class hierarchy, it is good practice to use the `final` keyword wherever possible; however, it is better to use a protocol-oriented design with value types to avoid this.

Swift's built-in types

If you are reading this book, you are probably very familiar with Swift's built-in data types and data structures. However, to really unleash their power, we need to understand how they are implemented in the Swift standard library. The Swift standard library defines several standard data types, such as Int, Double, and String. In most languages, these types are implemented as primitive types, which means that they cannot be extended or subclassed. In Swift, however, these types are implemented in the Swift standard library as structures, which means we can extend these types just as we can with any other type that is implemented as a structure; however, we cannot subclasses them as we can do with other languages.

 You can read more about Swift's standard library at `http://swiftdoc.org`

Swift also defines several standard data structures, such as arrays, dictionaries, and sets. Just like the built-in data types, these are also implemented as structures in the Swift standard library. You may be wondering about the performance of these data structures when they contain a large number of elements since value types receive a copy of the data structure when they are assigned to another variable. Apple has an answer for this, called **copy-on-write (COW)**.

COW

When an instance of a value type, such as a structure, is assigned to another variable, that second variable receives a copy of the instance. This means that if we had an array that contained 50,000 elements, then at runtime we would need to copy all 50,000 elements when we assigned the array to a second variable or if we passed it to another part of our code. This can severely impact our performance; however, with Swift built-in data structures such as the array, this impact is reduced because of COW.

With COW, Swift does not make a second copy of the data structure until a change is made to that data structure. Therefore, if we pass an array of 50,000 elements to another part of our code, and that code does not actually make any changes to the array, we will avoid the runtime overhead of copying all the elements.

Unfortunately, COW is only implemented with certain types in the Swift standard library and does not come free with all value types. In Chapter 4, *Generics*, we will look at how we can implement COW for our custom data types.

Summary

In most object-oriented programming languages, our type choices are limited. In Swift, however, we have numerous choices. This allows us to use the right type for the right situation. Understanding how the different types work is essential to writing good, stable code.

In this chapter, we looked at the different types we can use in Swift and emphasized the difference between value and reference types. Apple has said that value types should be preferred over reference types. We did look at areas, such as recursive data types, that require reference types.

We also discussed how we can optimize our code by using the `final` keyword when using reference types. In the next chapter, we will look at how we can avoid using a class hierarchy by using extensions.

3
Extensions

Back in the early 90s, when the primary language that I developed in was C, I had numerous custom libraries that contained functionality that was not a part of the standard C library. I found these libraries extremely useful because I tended to use the functionality they provided in most of my projects. This functionality included things such as converting the first letter of a character array to uppercase, or converting a numerical value to a currency string (two digits after the decimal point and a currency symbol). Having libraries such as these is extremely useful because there is always a functionality that we find useful that is not included in the standard library of the language we are developing in. I usually implemented this extra functionality in C with global functions. In more modern object-oriented languages, we can implement this functionality by subclassing the class we wish to add the functionality to; however, in Swift, we can use extensions to add this functionality to existing types without the need to use global functions or subclassing. To make extensions even more useful, Apple gave us the ability to extend protocols, which lets us add functionality to any type that adopts a protocol.

We will learn about the following topics in this chapter:

- How to extend structures, classes, and enumerations
- How to extend protocols
- How to use extensions in a real-world example

Extensions are one of the most useful features in the Swift language. They allow us to add functionality to an existing type even if we do not have the source code for the type. Protocol extensions are arguably one of the most exciting features of protocol-oriented programming. If you are not familiar with protocol extensions, you may be wondering how we can add functionality to a protocol when protocols do not contain any functionality. We will see how to use protocol extensions later in this chapter and see why they are so exciting. First, however, let's look at what extensions are and how to extend classes, structures, and enumerations.

With extensions, we can add the following items to an existing type:

- Computed properties
- Instance and type methods
- Convenience initializers
- Subscripts

One drawback of extensions is that we cannot override the functionality of the type we are extending. Extensions are designed to add additional functionality and are not designed as a means of changing the functionality of a type. Another thing that we cannot do with extensions is add stored properties; however, we can add computed properties.

To understand why extensions are so useful, we need to understand the problem that they are designed to solve. In most object-oriented languages, when we want to add additional functionality to an existing class, we generally subclass the class we want to add the extra functionality to. We then add the new functionality to this new subclass. The problem with this method is that we are not actually adding the functionality to the original class; therefore, we have to change all instances of the original class that need this extra functionality into instances of this new subclass. With some classes, such as the NSString class, it can take a significant amount of code to create a subclass.

Another problem we can run into is that we can only subclass reference types (classes). This means we are unable to subclass value types such as a structure or enumeration. What makes matters even worse is the fact that the greater part of the Swift standard library is made up of value types. This means that we are unable to add functionality to types from the Swift standard library by subclassing them. Apple has also recommended that we should prefer value types to reference types in our applications. Therefore, if we listen to Apple's recommendation (and we should), we cannot subclass the majority of our custom types.

With extensions, we are able to add new functionality directly to the types that we are extending. This means that all instances of that type automatically receive the new functionality without the need to change the type of the instance. We are also able to extend both reference and value types, which includes protocols. As we will see later in this chapter, the ability to extend protocols is one of the things that makes protocol-oriented programming possible.

Let's begin by looking at how we extend types such as structures, enumerations, and classes.

Defining an extension

An extension is defined by using the `extension` keyword, followed by the name of the type you are extending. We then put the functionality that we are adding to the type between curly brackets. The following example shows how to define an extension:

```
extension String {
    // Add functionality here
}
```

The previous example would add an extension to the `String` type from the Swift standard library. Since we can extend any type, we can use extensions to add functionality to types from the Swift standard library, types from frameworks, or our own custom types. While we can use extensions to add functionality to our own custom types, it is usually better to add the functionality directly to the type itself. The reason for this is that our code is easier to maintain if all the functionality (code) for our custom types is located together.

If we are adding functionality to a framework and we have the code for that framework, it is still better to add the functionality with an extension rather than changing the code within the framework itself. The reason for this is that if we add the functionality directly to the code within the framework, when we get newer versions of the framework, our changes will be overwritten. Newer versions of the framework will not overwrite our extensions as long as we do not put them in a file that belongs to the framework.

Let's see how we can add functionality to a standard Swift type using an extension. The following code extends the `String` type to add a method that returns an optional value that contains either the third character of the string or `nil`, if the string is empty:

```
extension String  {
    func getThirdChar() -> Character? {
        guard self.count > 2 else {
            return  nil
        }
        return self[self.index(self.startIndex, offsetBy: 2)]
    }
}
```

Once we add this extension to our application, all instances of the `String` type can take advantage of the new functionality. There is also nothing special that needs to be done to access the functionality; instances of the `String` type do not know or care whether the functionality came from the original implementation of the type or from an extension.

The following example shows how we use the `getThirdChar()` method:

```
var myString = "This is a test"
print(myString.getThirdChar())
```

The previous example will print the character `i` to the console. It is just as easy to add other functionality, such as subscripts, to existing types. The following example shows how we would add a subscript to our `String` extension that accepts a range operator and returns a substring with the characters defined by the range operator:

```
extension String {
    func getThirdChar() -> Character? {
        guard self.count > 2 else {
            return nil
        }
        return self[self.index(self.startIndex, offsetBy: 2)]
    }
    subscript (r: CountableClosedRange<Int>) -> String? {
        get {
            let start = index(self.startIndex, offsetBy:r.lowerBound,
                              limitedBy: endIndex)
            let end = index(self.startIndex, offsetBy:r.upperBound,
                            limitedBy: endIndex)
            if let start = start, let end = end {
                return String(self[start ..< end])
            }
            return nil
        }
    }
}
```

In `Chapter 2`, *Our Type Choices*, we mentioned that types that are normally implemented as primitives in other languages are implemented as named types in Swift. These include types that represent numbers, characters, and Boolean values. Since they are implemented as named types, we are also able to extend them as we would any other type. As an example, if we wanted to extend the Integer type to add a method that would return the value of the integer squared, we could do it with an extension such as this:

```
extension Int  {
    func squared() -> Int  {
        return self * self
    }
}
```

We could then use this extension to get the value of any integer squared, as shown in the following example:

```
print(21.squared())
```

Another example would be to extend the `Double` type, in order to add a method that would convert the value of the double to a `String` type representing the value as a currency. This method would round the number to two decimal places and add a currency symbol. The following code demonstrates how we could do this:

```
extension Double {
    func currencyString() -> String {
        let divisor = pow(10.0, 2.0)
        let num = (self  *  divisor).rounded() / divisor
        return "$\(num)"
    }
}
```

We cannot add stored properties with extensions; however, we can add computed properties. Earlier in this section, we added a method named `squared()` to the `Integer` type. We could have implemented this functionality as a computed property, as shown in the following example:

```
extension Int {
    var squared: Int {
        return self * self
    }
}
```

Now that we have seen how to extend a standard type such as classes, enumerations, or structures, let's see what **protocol extensions** are all about.

Protocol extensions

Protocols, like other types, can be extended. Protocol extensions can be used to provide common functionality to all types that conform to a particular protocol. This gives us the ability to add functionality to any type that conforms to a protocol rather than adding the functionality to each individual type or through a global function. Protocol extensions, like regular extensions, also give us the ability to add functionality to types for which we do not have the source code.

Protocol-oriented programming and frameworks such as **GameplayKit** rely heavily on protocol extensions. Without protocol extensions, if we wanted to add specific functionality to a group of types that conformed to a protocol, we would have to add the functionality to each of the types. If we were using reference types (classes), we could create a class hierarchy, but, as we mentioned earlier, that is not possible with value types. Apple has stated that we should prefer value types to reference types, and, in with protocol extensions, we have the ability to add common functionality to a group of values and/or reference types that conform to a specific protocol, without having to implement that functionality in all types.

Let's see what protocol extensions can do for us. The Swift standard library provides a protocol named **Collection**: http://swiftdoc.org/nightly/protocol/Collection/.

This protocol inherits from the Sequence protocol and is adopted by all of Swift's standard collection types, such as the Dictionary and Array.

Let's say that we wanted to add the functionality to all types that conform to the Collection protocol. This new functionality would return only the items whose index number is an even number. We could very easily add this functionality by extending the Collection protocol, as shown in the following code:

```
extension Collection {
    func evenElements() -> [Iterator.Element] {

        var index = startIndex
        var result: [Iterator.Element] = []
        var i = 0
        repeat {
            if i % 2 == 0 {
                result.append(self[index])
            }
            index = self.index(after: index)
            i += 1
        } while (index != endIndex)
        return result
    }
}
```

Notice that when we extend a protocol, we use the same syntax and format that we use when we extend other types. We use the `extension` keyword followed by the name of the protocol that we are extending. We then put the functionality that we are adding between the curly brackets. Now, every type that conforms to the `Collection` protocol will receive the `evenElements()` functions. The following code shows how we would use these functions with an array:

```
var origArray = [1,2,3,4,5,6,7,8,9,10]
var newArray = origArray.evenElements()
```

In the previous code, the `newArray` array will contain the elements 1, 3, 5, 7, and 9, because those elements have index numbers that are even (we are looking at the index number, not the value of the element).

Protocol extensions are great for adding functionality to a group of types without the need to add the code to each of the individual types; however, it is important to know what types conform to the protocol we are extending. In the previous example, we extended the `Collection` protocol by adding the `evenElements()` methods to all types that conform to the protocol. One of the types that conforms to this protocol is the `Dictionary` type. However, the `Dictionary` type is an unordered collection; therefore, the `evenElements()` method will not work as expected. The following example illustrates this:

```
var origDict = [1:"One",2:"Two",3:"Three",4:"Four"]
var returnElements = origDict.evenElements()
for item in returnElements  {
    print(item)
}
```

Since the `Dictionary` type does not promise to store the items in any particular order, any of the two items could be printed to the screen in this example. The following shows one possible output from this code:

```
(2, "two")
(1, "One")
```

Another problem is that anyone who is not familiar with how the `evenElements()` method is implemented may expect the `returnElements` array to be of the `Dictionary` type since the original collection is a `Dictionary` type; however, it is actually an instance of the `Array` type. This can cause some confusion. Therefore, we need to be careful when we extend a protocol to make sure the functionality we are adding works as expected for all types that conform to the protocol.

In the case of the evenElements() methods, we might have been better served by adding the functionality as an extension directly to the Array type rather than the Collection protocol. However, there is another way. We can add constraints to our extensions that will limit the types that receive the functionality defined in an extension.

In order for a type to receive the functionality defined in a protocol extension, it must satisfy all constraints defined within the protocol extension. A constraint is added after the name of the protocol that we are extending using the where keyword. The following example shows how we would add a constraint to our Collection extension:

```
extension Collection where Self: ExpressibleByArrayLiteral {
    //Extension code here
}
```

In the Collection protocol extensions in the previous example, only types that also conform to the ExpressibleByArrayLiteral protocol (http://swiftdoc.org/nightly/protocol/ExpressibleByArrayLiteral/) will receive the functionality defined in the extension. Since the Dictionary type does not conform to the ExpressibleByArrayLiteral protocol, it will not receive the functionality defined within the protocol extension.

We could also use constraints to specify that our Collection protocol extension only applies to a collection whose elements conform to a specific protocol. In the following example, we use constraints to make sure that the elements in the collection conform to the Comparable protocol. This may be necessary if the functionality that we are adding relies on the ability to compare two or more elements in the collection. We could add this constraint as follows:

```
extension Collection where Iterator.Element: Comparable  {
    // Add functionality here
}
```

Constraints give us the ability to limit which types receive the functionality defined in the extension. One thing that we need to be careful of is using protocol extensions when we should actually be extending an individual type. Protocol extensions should be used when we want to add functionality to a group of types. If we are trying to add the functionality to a single type, we should look to extend that individual type.

Now that we have seen how to use extensions and protocol extensions, let's look at a real-world example. In this example, we will demonstrate how to create a **text validation** framework.

Text validation

In numerous apps across multiple platforms (iOS, Android, and Windows), I have been tasked to validate user input either after the user has entered it or as it is entered. This validation can be done very easily with regular expressions. However, we do not want various regular expression strings littered throughout our code. We can solve this problem by creating different classes or structures that contain the validation code. The question is, how would we organize these types to make them easy to use and maintain? Prior to the protocol extensions in Swift, I would have used protocols to define the validation requirements and would then create a type that conforms to the protocol for each validation type needed.

Prior to looking at how we would accomplish this text validation, let's take a quick look at what **regular expressions** are and how we would use them in Swift. A regular expression (also known as a **regex**) is a special text string that is used to describe a search or matching pattern. The regular expression string, also known as a pattern, consists of one or more characters, operators, or constructs. Regular expressions are very useful when searching for a string for a particular pattern or (as we use it here) validating a string.

Regular expressions are not unique to Swift. Almost all modern languages have a way to use regular expressions. Whole books have been written about regular expressions, so, in this section, we will give a very brief introduction with enough information for you to understand the examples in this chapter.

In its simplest form, a regular expression is a string of characters, such as abc or 12345. Using a regular expression such as this will match the pattern within a string, as shown in the following examples:

Regex	Matches	Description
abc	xyzabcxyzabc	Matches the abc string.
12345	1234567890	Matches the 12345 string.

We can also define character sets using square brackets ([]). Character sets will match one character in the string to any character within the set. To define the set, we can use a string of characters, as shown in the previous example, or we can use the minus sign (-) operator to specify a range:

Regex	Matches	Description
[abc]	xyzabcxyz	Matches any character in the abc set.
[a-zA-Z]	xyzabcxyz	Matches any lower or uppercase letter.

We use curly brackets ({}) to specify the amount of repetition, so we can match more than one character. For example, if we used {2,5}, then that would mean we want to match at least two characters, but no more than five characters:

Regex	Matches	Description
[a-z]{2,5}	xyzabcxyz	Matches two to five lowercase letters.
[a-z0-9]{2,5}	xyzabcxyz	Matches two to five lowercase letters or numbers.

The caret (^) at the beginning means we want to match at the beginning, and the dollar sign ($) means match at the end. We can use these two special characters to match a full string. For example, the ^[a-z]{0,5}$ pattern will match a string only if there are between zero and five lowercase letters. The match will fail if there are any other characters besides lowercase letters or more than five characters:

Regex	Matches	Description
^[a-z]{2,5}$	xyzabcxyz	Fails more than five characters.
[a-z0-9]{0,5}	xyz12	Matches five lowercase or number characters.

Finally, let's look at some additional special characters within regular expressions. These are characters that need to be escaped using the backslash (\) and have special meaning:

Character	Definition
.	Matches any single character.
\n	Matches a newline character.
\t	Matches a tab.
\d	Matches a digit [0-9].
\D	Matches a non-digit.
\w	Matches an alphanumeric character [a-zA-Z0-9].
\W	Matches a non-alphanumeric character.
\s	Matches a whitespace character.
\S	Matches a non-whitespace character.

There is a lot more to regular expressions than we have just seen. In this section, we only gave enough information to help you understand the text validation examples in this chapter. If you plan on using regular expressions on a regular (pun intended) basis, I would suggest reading more about them.

Now, let's look at how we would develop our validation framework without protocol extensions. We will begin by defining a protocol named `TextValidation` that will define the requirements for any type used for text validation. This will allow us to use the `TextValidation` protocol in place of implementation types. If you recall, this is a form of polymorphism:

```
protocol TextValidation {

    var regExMatchingString: String {get}
    var regExFindMatchString: String {get}
    var validationMessage: String {get}

    func validateString(str: String) -> Bool
    func getMatchingString(str: String) -> String?
}
```

In this protocol, we define three properties and two methods that any type that conforms to this protocol must implement. The three properties are as follows:

- `regExMatchingString`: A regular expression string used to verify that the input string contains only valid characters.
- `regExFindMatchString`: A regular expression string used to retrieve a new string from the input string that contains only valid characters. This regular expression is generally used when we need to validate the input in real time, as the user enters information, because it will remove all characters, starting with the first invalid characters to the end of the string.
- `validationMessage`: This is the error message to display whether the input string contained non-valid characters.

The two methods for this protocol are as follows:

- `validateString`: This method will return true if the input string contains only valid characters. The `regExMatchingString` property will be used in this method to perform the match.
- `getMatchingString`: This method will return a new string that contains only valid characters. This method is generally used when we need to validate the input in real time, as the user enters information, because it will remove all characters starting with the first invalid characters. We will use the `regExFindMatchString` property in this method to retrieve the new string.

Now, let's see how we would create a class that conforms to this protocol. The following class would be used to verify that the input string contains 0 to 10 alpha characters:

```
class AlphabeticValidation1: TextValidation {
    static let sharedInstance = AlphabeticValidation1()
    private init(){}
    let regExFindMatchString = "^[a-zA-Z]{0,10}"
    let validationMessage = "Can only contain Alpha characters"
    var regExMatchingString: String {
        get {
            return regExFindMatchString + "$"
        }
    }
    func validateString(str: String) -> Bool {
        if let _ = str.range(of: regExMatchingString,
                             options: .regularExpression){
            return   true
        } else {
            return   false
        }
    }
    func getMatchingString(str: String) -> String? {
        if let newMatch = str.range(of: regExFindMatchString,
                                    options: .regularExpression) {
            return String(str[newMatch])
        } else {
            return nil
        }
    }
}
```

In this implementation, the `regExFindMatchString` and `validationMessage` properties are stored properties, and the `regExMatchingString` property is a computed property. We also implement the `validateString()` and `getMatchingString()` methods within the class to conform to the protocol.

Normally, we would have several different types that conform to the `TextValidation` protocol where each one would validate a different type of input. As we can see from the `AlphabeticValidation1` class, there would be quite a bit of code involved with each validation type. The worst part is that a lot of the code would need to be duplicated for each validation type. This is not ideal. However, if we wanted to avoid creating a class hierarchy with a superclass containing the duplicate code, we would have no other choice. Protocol extensions give us a better option. Let's look at how we would implement our text validation types with protocol extensions.

With protocol extensions, we need to think about the code a little differently. The big difference is that we do not need, nor want to define, everything in the protocol. With standard protocols, or when we use a class hierarchy, all methods and properties that we want to access, using the interface provided by the generic superclass or protocol type, must be defined within the superclass or protocol. With protocol extensions, it is actually preferable for us to not define a computed property or method in the protocol if we are going to implement it with a protocol extension. Therefore, when we rewrite our text validation types with protocol extensions, the TextValidation protocol would be greatly simplified and would look like this:

```
protocol TextValidation {
    var regExFindMatchString: String {get}
    var validationMessage: String {get}
}
```

In the original TextValidation protocol, we defined three properties and two methods. As we can see in this new protocol, we are only defining two properties. Now that we have the TextValidation protocol defined, let's create a protocol extension where we implement the other two methods and the computed property:

```
extension TextValidation {
    var regExMatchingString: String {
        get {
            return regExFindMatchString + "$"
        }
    }
    func validateString(str: String) -> Bool {
        if let _ = str.range(of: regExMatchingString,
                            options: .regularExpression){
            return true
        } else {
            return false
        }
    }
    func getMatchingString(str: String) -> String? {
        if let newMatch = str.range(of: regExFindMatchString,
                                options: .regularExpression){
            return String(str[newMatch])
        } else {
            return nil
        }
    }
}
```

In the `TextValidation` protocol extension, we implement the two methods and the computed property that were defined in the original `TextValidation` protocol, but are not defined in the new one.

Now that we have created our protocol and protocol extension, we are able to define our text validation types. In the following code, we define three classes that we will use to validate text:

```
class AlphabeticValidation: TextValidation {
    static let sharedInstance = AlphabeticValidation()
    private init(){}
    let regExFindMatchString = "^[a-zA-Z]{0,10}"
    let validationMessage = "Can only contain Alpha characters"
}

class AlphaNumericValidation: TextValidation {
    static let sharedInstance = AlphaNumericValidation()
    private init(){}
    let regExFindMatchString = "^[a-zA-Z0-9]{0,15}"
    let validationMessage = "Can only contain Alpha Numeric
                            characters"
}

class DisplayNameValidation: TextValidation {
    static let sharedInstance = DisplayNameValidation()
    private init(){}
    let regExFindMatchString = "^[\\s?[a-zA-Z0-9\\-_\\s]]{0,15}"
    let validationMessage = "Display Name can contain only contain
                            Alphanumeric Characters"
}
```

In each of the text validation classes, we create a static constant and a private initiator so we can use the class as a singleton. For more information on the singleton pattern, please see *The singleton design pattern* section of Chapter 8, *Adopting Design Patterns in Swift*.

After we define the singleton pattern, all we do for each type is set the values for the `regExFindMatchString` and `validationMessage` properties. Now, we have virtually no duplicate code between the types, except the code to implement the singleton pattern. Even if we could, we would not want to define the singleton code in the protocol extension because we would not want to force that pattern on all conforming types. We can also see that we are able to define these three classes with less code than it took to define the one class without protocol extensions.

We could use these `validation` classes as follows:

```
var myString1 = "abcxyz"
var myString2 = "abc123"
var validation = AlphabeticValidation.sharedInstance

validation.validateString(str: myString1)
validation.validateString(str: myString2)

validation.getMatchingString(str: myString1)
validation.getMatchingString(str: myString2)
```

In this example, we create two `String` types, each containing a different string value. We then get the shared instance of the `AlphabeticValidation` type. We use the `validateString()` method of the `AlphabeticValidation` instance to validate the strings, which verifies that the whole string matches the regular expression pattern defined in the `AlphabeticValidation` instance. We then use the `getMatchingString()` method of the `AlphabeticValidation` instance to return a new string that contains only the valid characters defined in the regular expression pattern.

The `validateString()` method returns a true value for the `myString1` string because the value of `myString1` matches the regular expression pattern. However, it returns a false value for the `myString2` instances because their value contains numbers that do not match the `^[a-zA-Z]{0,10}` regular expression pattern defined in the `AlphabeticValidation` type.

The `getMatchingString()` method returns the full value of the `myString1` string because the value matches the regular expression pattern defined in the `AlphabeticValidation` type. However, for the value of the `myString2` instance, it only returns an instance of the `String` type that contains the value of `abc` because that is the only part of the `myString2` value that matches the pattern.

As we mentioned in `Chapter 2`, *Our Type Choices*, it is important to understand that the majority of the Swift standard library is made up of structures (value types) and protocols. In this next section, we will see why that is so important.

Extensions with the Swift standard library

Let's say that, in our application, we needed to calculate the factorial of some integers. A factorial is written as 5!. To calculate a factorial, we take the product of all the positive integers that are less than, or equal to, the number. The following example shows how we would calculate the factorial of five:

```
5!  =   5*4*3*2*1
5!  =   120
```

We could very easily create a global function to calculate the factorial, and we would do that in most languages. However, in Swift, extensions give us a better way to do this. The Integer type in Swift is implemented as a structure that we can extend to add this functionality directly to the type itself. The following example shows how we can do this:

```
extension Int {
    func factorial() -> Int {
        var answer = 1
        for x in (1...self).reversed() {
            answer *= x
        }
        return answer
    }
}
```

We could now calculate the factorial of any integer as follows:

```
print(10.factorial())
```

If we run this code, we will see that the correct answer of 3,628,800 is returned. In this example, we also see how easy it is to extend a type to add extra functionality even if we do not have the code for the type.

If we will be doing a lot of comparison of our custom types, it is a good idea to have them conform to the Equatable protocol. In the next section, we will see how we can do this with extensions.

Conforming to the Equatable protocol

In this section, we will show how we can conform to the Equatable protocol using extensions. When a type conforms to the Equatable protocol, we can use the equal-to (==) operator to compare for equality, and the not-equal-to (!=) operator to compare for inequality.

If you are comparing instances of a custom type, it is a good idea to have that type conform to the Equatable protocol because it makes comparing instances very easy.

Let's start off by creating the type that we will compare. We will name this type Place:

```
struct Place {
    let id: String
    let latitude: Double
    let longitude: Double
}
```

In the Place type, we have three properties, which represent the ID of the place and the latitude and longitude coordinates for its location. If there are two instances of the Place type that have the same ID and coordinates, then they would be considered the same place.

To implement the Equatable protocol, we could create a global function. However, that is not the recommended solution for protocol-oriented programming. We could also add a static function to the Place type itself, but sometimes, it is better to pull the functionality needed to conform to a protocol out of the implementation itself. The following code would make the Place type conform to the Equatable protocol:

```
extension Place: Equatable {
    static func ==(lhs: Place, rhs: Place) -> Bool {
        return lhs.id == rhs.id && lhs.latitude ==
        rhs.latitude && lhs.longitude ==
        rhs.longitude
    }
}
```

We can now compare instances of the Place type like this:

```
var placeOne = Place(id: "Fenway Park", latitude: 42.3467,
                longitude: -71.0972)var placeTwo = Place(id: "Wrigley
                Field", latitude: 41.9484, longitude: -87.6553)

print(placeOne == placeTwo)
```

This would print **false**, because Fenway Park and Wrigley Field are two different baseball stadiums.

You may be wondering why we said that it may be better to pull the functionality needed to conform to a protocol out of the implementation itself. Think about some of the larger types that you have created in the past. Personally, I have seen types that had several hundred lines of code and conformed to numerous protocols. By pulling the code that is needed to conform to a protocol out of the type's implementation and putting it in its own extension, we are making our code much easier to read and maintain in the future because the implementation code is isolated in its own extension.

Summary

In this chapter, we looked at extensions and protocol extensions. In the original version of Swift, we were able to use extensions to extend structures, classes, and enumerations, but since Swift 2, we have also been able to use extensions to extend protocols.

Without protocol extensions, protocol-oriented programming would not be possible, but we need to make sure that we use protocol extensions where appropriate and do not try to use them where regular extensions should be used.

In the next chapter, we will look at the final piece of the protocol-oriented puzzle: **generics**.

4
Generics

I received a lot of feedback about protocol-oriented programming after the first version of this book was released. Almost all the feedback was very positive; however, there was one conversation that I had—with one of the smartest people that I have had the privilege to meet—about what protocol-oriented programming was. One of the comments he made was that I should not forget about **generic programming**. The conversation we had about generic programming really stuck with me and when I had the opportunity to write a new version of this book, I took the opportunity to include this chapter on generics.

In this chapter, we will learn about the following:

- What generics are
- How to create generic functions
- How to create generic types
- How to use generic subscripts
- How to implement **copy-on-write** (**COW**)
- How to design flexible and reusable types with protocols and generics

Generics allow us to write very flexible and reusable code that avoids duplication. With a type-safe language, such as Swift, we often need to write functions or types that are valid for multiple types. For example, we might need to write a function that swaps the values of two variables; however, we may want this function to swap two string types, two integer types, and two double types. Without generics, we would need to write three separate functions. With generics, we can write one generic function to provide the swap functionality for different types.

> *Generics allow us to tell a function or type, "I know Swift is a type-safe language, but I do not know the type that will be needed yet. I will give you a placeholder for now and will let you know what type to enforce at runtime."*

Whether you realize it or not, generics play a very large part in every program written in Swift because generics play such a large part in the Swift language itself. We can look at arrays as an example of where generics are used in the Swift standard library. Generics allow us to create an array that contains instances of any type.

Optionals are another example of where generics are used in the Swift language. The Optional type is defined as an enumeration with two possible values: None and Some(T), where T is the associated value of the appropriate type. If we set the optional to nil, then it will have a value of None, and if we set a value for the optional, then it will have a value of Some with an associated value of the appropriate type. Internally, an optional is defined as follows:

```
enum Optional<T>{
    case None
    case Some(T)
}
```

Here, T is the type associated with the optional. The T placeholder is used to define generics. As we will see later in this chapter, we are not limited to using just the T as a placeholder, but for most of the examples in this chapter, we will use either T or E to represent a generic type because those are the standard placeholders used in most documentation to represent a generic type.

In Swift, we have the ability to define both generic functions and generic types. Let's start by looking at how we would create a generic function.

Generic functions

To fully understand generics, we need to understand the problem that they are designed to solve. Let's say that we wanted to create functions that swapped the values of two variables (as described in the first part of this chapter); however, for our application, we need to swap the instances of two Integer types, two Double types, and two String types. Without generics, this would require us to write the following three functions:

```
func swapInts (a: inout Int, b: inout Int)  {
    let tmp = a
    a = b
    b = tmp
}

func swapDoubles(a: inout Double, b: inout Double)  {
    let tmp = a
    a = b
```

```
        b = tmp
}

func swapStrings(a: inout String, b: inout String)  {
    let tmp = a
    a = b
    b = tmp
}
```

With these three functions, we can swap the instances of two Integer types, two Double types, and two String types. Now, let's say that, as we develop our application further, we find out that we also need to swap the values of two UInt32 types, two float types, or even a couple of custom types. We could easily end up with eight or nine swap functions. The worst part is that each of those functions would contain duplicate code because the only difference between them would be the parameter types. While this solution does work, generics offer a much more elegant and simple solution that eliminates all the duplicate code. Let's see how we would condense all three of the preceding functions into a single generic function:

```
func swapGeneric<T>(a: inout T, b: inout T)  {
    let tmp = a
    a = b
    b = tmp
}
```

Let's look at how we defined the swapGeneric(a:b:) function. The function itself looks pretty similar to a normal function, except for the capital T placeholder used in the function definition. This placeholder tells Swift that we will be defining the type at runtime. We can then use that placeholder type in place of any type definition within the parameter definitions, the return type, or the function itself. The big thing to keep in mind is that, once the placeholder is defined as a type, all the other placeholders assume that type. Therefore, any variable or constant defined with that placeholder must be an instance of that type.

There is nothing special about the capital T; we could use any valid identifier in place of it. The following definitions are perfectly valid:

```
func swapGeneric<G>(a: inout G, b: inout   G)  {
    //Statements
}

func swapGeneric<xyz>(a: inout xyz, b: inout xyz)  {
    //Statements
}
```

In most documentation, generic placeholders are defined with either T (for type) or E (for element). For standard purposes, we will use T to define most generic placeholders in this chapter. Another good practice is to use T to define a generic placeholder within our code so that the placeholder is easily recognizable when we are looking at the code.

Let's look at how we would call a generic function. The following code swaps two integers:

```
var a = 5
var b = 10
swapGeneric(a: &a, b: &b)
print("a: \(a)   b: \(b)")
```

If we run this code, the output will be: a: 10 b: 5. We can see that we do not have to do anything special to call a generic function. The function infers the type from the first parameter and then sets all the remaining placeholders to that type. Now, if we needed to swap the values of two String types, we could use the same function as follows:

```
var c = "My String 1"
var d = "My String 2"
swapGeneric(a: &c, b: &d)
print("c:\(c)   d:\(d)")
```

We can see that we call the function in exactly the same way as we called it when we wanted to swap two integers. One thing that we cannot do is pass two different types into the swapGeneric() function because we only defined one generic placeholder. If we attempt to run the following code, we will receive an error:

```
var a = 5
var c = "My string 1"
swapGeneric(a: &a, b: &c)
```

The error that we would receive is: cannot convert the value of the String type to the expected argument of the Integer type, which tells us that we are attempting to use a String type where an Integer type is expected. The reason that the function is looking for an Integer value is because the first parameter that we passed into the function was an instance of the Integer type; therefore, all the generic types in the function defined with the T placeholder become Integer types.

If we need to use multiple generic types, we can create multiple placeholders by separating them with commas. The following example shows us how to define multiple placeholders for a single function:

```
func testGeneric<T,E>(a:T, b:E)  {
    print("\(a) \(b)")
}
```

In this example, we are defining two generic placeholders, `T` and `E`. In this case, we can set the `T` placeholder to one type and the `E` placeholder to a different type.

This function will accept parameters of different types; however, since they are of different types, we would be unable to swap the values. There are also other limitations on generics. For example, we may think that the following generic function would be valid; however, we would receive an error if we tried to implement it:

```
func genericEqual<T>(a: T, b: T)  ->  Bool{
    return a == b
}
```

The error that we receive is the `binaryoperator'=='cannotbeappliedtotwo'T'` operand. Since the type of the argument is unknown at the time the code is compiled, Swift does not know if it is able to use the equal operator on the type, which causes the error to be thrown. We might think that this is a limit that would make generics hard to use; however, we have a way to tell Swift that we expect that the type will have a certain functionality. This is done with type constraints.

Type constraints with generics

A type constraint specifies that a generic type must inherit from a specific class or conform to a particular protocol. This allows us to use the methods or properties defined by the parent class or protocol with the generic types. Let's look at how to use type constraints by rewriting the `genericEqual()` function to use the `Comparable` protocol:

```
func testGenericComparable<T: Comparable>(a: T, b: T) -> Bool {
    return a == b
}
```

To specify the type constraint, we put the type or protocol constraint after the generic placeholder, thus separating the generic placeholder and the constraint with a colon. This new function works in ways that we might expect it to, and it will compare the values of the two parameters and return `true` if they are equal, or `false` if they are not.

We can declare multiple constraints, just like we can declare multiple generic types. The following example shows us how to declare two generic types with different constraints:

```
func testFunction<T: MyClass, E: MyProtocol>(a: T, b: E) {
}
```

In this function, the type defined by the `T` placeholder must inherit from the `MyClass` class, and the type defined by the `E` placeholder must implement the `MyProtocol` protocol. Now that we have looked at generic functions and type constraints, let's look at generic types.

Generic types

A generic type is a class, structure, or enumeration that can work with any type, just like how Swift arrays and optionals can work with any type. When we create an instance of our generic type, we specify the type that the instance will work with. Once a type is defined, the type cannot be changed for that instance.

To demonstrate how to create a generic type, let's create a simple `List` class. This class will use a Swift array as the backend storage and will let us add items or retrieve values from the list.

Let's begin by seeing how to define our generic `List` type:

```
struct List<T> {
}
```

The preceding code defines the generic `List` type. We can see that we use the `<T>` tag to define a generic placeholder, just like we did when we defined a generic function. This `T` placeholder can then be used anywhere within the type instead of a concrete type definition.

To create an instance of this type, we would need to define the type of items that our list will hold. The following examples show us how to create instances of the generic `List` type for various types:

```
var stringList = List<String>()
var intList = List<Int>()
var customList = List<MyObject>()
```

The preceding example creates three instances of the `List` type. The `stringList` instance can be used with instances of the String type, the `intList` instance can be used with instances of the Integer type, and the `customList` instance can be used with instances of the `MyObject` type.

We are not limited to using generics only with structures. We can also define classes and enumerations as generic types. The following examples show us how to define a generic structure and a generic enumeration:

```
class GenericStruct<T> {
}

enum GenericEnum<T> {
}
```

The next step in our List type is to add the backend storage array. The items that are stored in this array need to be of the same type as we define when we initiate the class; therefore, we will use the T placeholder for the array's definition. The following code shows the List class with a named items array:

```
struct List<T> {
    var items = [T]()
}
```

Now, we will need to add the add(item:) method that will be used to add an item to the list. We will use the T placeholder within the method declaration to define that the parameter will be of the same type as we declared when we initiated the type. Therefore, if we create an instance of the List type that will use the String type, we will be required to use the String type as the parameter for this method.

Here is the code for the add() function:

```
mutating func add(item: T) {
    items.append(item)
}
```

When we created a standalone generic function, we added the <T> declaration after the function name to declare that it was a generic function. When we use a generic method within a generic type, we do not need this declaration because we already specified that the type itself is generic with the T type. To define a generic method within a generic type, all we need to do is to use the same placeholder that we defined in the type declaration.

Now, let's add the getItemAtIndex(index:) method, which will return an item from the backend array at the specified index:

```
func getItemAtIndex(index: Int) -> T? {
    guard index < items.count else {
        return nil
    }
    return items
}
```

The getItemAtIndex(index:) method accepts one argument, the index of the item we want to retrieve. We then use the T placeholder with the return type. The return type for this method is an optional type that might be of type T or might be nil. If the backend storage array contains an item at the specified index, we will return that item, otherwise, we will return nil.

Now, let's look at our entire generic list class:

```
struct List<T> {
    var items = [T]()
    mutating func add(item:  T)  {
        items.append(item)
    }

    func getItemAtIndex(index: Int) -> T? {
        if items.count > index {
            return items[index]
        } else {
        return nil
        }
    }
}
```

As you can see, we initially defined the generic T placeholder type in the structure's declaration. We then used that placeholder type within the structure in three places. We used the placeholder as the type for our items array, as the parameter type for the add(index:) method, and as the value for the optional return type in the getItemAtIndex() method.

Now, let's look at how to use the List class. When we use a generic type, we define the type to be used within the instance between angle brackets. The following code shows how to use the List class to store String types:

```
var list = List<String>()
list.add(item: "Hello")
list.add(item: "World")
print(list.getItemAtIndex(index: 1))
```

In this code, we start off by creating an instance of the List type called list and define that it will store String types. We then use the add(index:) method twice to store two items in the list instance. Finally, we use the getItemAtIndex() method to retrieve the item at index number 1, which will display Optional(World) to the console.

At the end of this chapter, we will look at the `List` type again and show you how to design and develop a `List` type in a protocol-oriented way with the COW feature.

We can also define our generic types with multiple placeholder types, similar to how we use multiple placeholders in our generic methods. To use multiple placeholder types, we will separate them with commas. The following example shows how to define multiple placeholder types:

```
class MyClass<T,E>{
}
```

We then create an instance of the `MyClass` type that uses instances of the `String` and `Integer` types, like this:

```
var mc = MyClass<String, Int>()
```

Type constraints can also be used with generic types. Once again, using a type constraint for a generic type is exactly the same as using one with a generic function. The following code shows how to use a type constraint to ensure that the generic type conforms to the comparable protocol:

```
struct MyStruct<T: Comparable>{}
```

So far, in this chapter, we have seen how to use placeholder types with functions and types; however, this book is about protocol-oriented programming. When we declare generic types in a protocol, they are known as associated types.

Associated types

An associated type declares a placeholder name that can be used instead of a type within a protocol. The actual type to be used is not specified until the protocol itself is adopted. When creating generic functions and types, we used a very similar syntax to what we have seen throughout this chapter. Defining associated types for a protocol, however, is a little different. We specify an associated type using the `associatedtype` keyword.

Let's see how to use associated types when we define a protocol. For this example, we will create a simple protocol named `MyProtocol`:

```
protocol MyProtocol {
    associatedtype E
    var items: [E] {get set}
    mutating func add(item: E)
}
```

In this protocol, we declare an associated type named `E`. We then use that associated type as the type for the `items` array, as well as the parameter type for the `add(item:)` method.

We can now create types that conform to this protocol by providing either a concrete type or a generic type for the associated type. Let's see how we could create a type that conforms to the `MyProtocol` protocol using a concrete type:

```
struct MyIntType: MyProtocol {
    var items: [Int] = []
    mutating func add(item: Int) {
        items.append(item)
    }
}
```

In this code, we create a type named `MyIntType` that conforms to the `MyProtocol` protocol. We then implement the items array and the `add(item:)` method using the integer type. Swift recognizes that we are using the integer type in place of the associated type; therefore, we do need to make sure we use the same type wherever the associated type was used. Now, let's see how we would use a generic type when creating a type that conforms to the `MyProtocol` protocol:

```
struct MyGenericType<T>: MyProtocol {
    var items: [T] = []
    mutating func add(item:  T) {
        items.append(item)
    }
}
```

This code should look very familiar, as it is very similar to how we created a generic type. The `T` placeholder is used wherever the associated type is used in the protocol, and when we create an instance of the `MyGenericType` type, we will need to define what type to use.

Let's look at the generic subscripts that were added to Swift in version 4.

Generic subscripts

Prior to Swift version 4, we could use generics with subscripts only if the generic type was defined in the containing type; however, we were unable to define a new generic type within the subscript definition. For example, if we had a `List` type, we could use the generic type defined by the `List` type within the subscript, as shown in this example:

```
struct List<T> {
    /*  other implementation code here */
```

```
subscript(index: Int) -> T? {
    return getItemAtIndex(index: index)
}
}
```

With Swift version 4 and later, we are able to define generic types within the subscript definition itself. To see how we would do this, let's go ahead and create another very basic generic `List` type. The following code shows us how to do this:

```
struct List<T> {
    private var items = [T]()
    public mutating func add(item: T) {
        items.append(item)
    }
    public func getItemAtIndex(index: Int) -> T? {
        if items.count > index {
            return items[index]
        } else {
            return nil
        }
    }
    public subscript(index: Int) -> T? {
        return getItemAtIndex(index: index)
    }
}
```

This `List` type gives us the very basic functionality of adding an item to the end of the list and retrieving an item at a specific index. We would obviously need additional functionality to make a functional `List` type, but for our example, this is enough to show us how a generic subscript works.

Now, let's say that we have a requirement to retrieve a range of elements from the list using a subscript. With generic subscripts, we can do this very easily with the following code:

```
public subscript<E: Sequence>(indices: E) -> [T] where E.Iterator.Element
== Int {
    var result = [T]()
    for index in indices {
        result.append(items[index])
    }
    return result
}
```

This subscript will take a sequence of indices and will return an array containing the values at each index. We define a generic type (E) that must conform to the Sequence protocol and then use that type as the parameter for the subscript. With the where clause, we are requiring the elements in the iterator, within the E type, to be of the Integer type.

We can now use the subscript, as shown in the following code:

```
var myList = List<Int>()
myList.add(item: 1)
myList.add(item: 2)
myList.add(item: 3)
myList.add(item: 4)
myList.add(item: 5)

var values = myList[2...4]
```

In this code, we create an instance of the List type and specify that it will contain instances of the Integer type. We then add five values to the list. In the last line, we use the subscript that we just added to the List type to retrieve an array that contains the values at indices of two, three, and four. The values array will contain the last three elements of the list instance.

In Chapter 2, *Our Type Choices*, we briefly mentioned COW. At that time, we mentioned that Apple provided the COW feature for some of the types in the Swift standard library. Let's look at this feature again and see how we can add it to our custom types.

COW

Normally, when we pass an instance of a value type, such as a structure, we create a new copy of the instance. This means that if we had a large data structure that contained 50,000 elements, every time we passed that instance, we would have to copy all 50,000 elements. This could have a detrimental impact on the performance of our applications, especially if we passed that instance to numerous functions.

To solve this issue, Apple has implemented the COW feature for all the data structures (array, dictionary, and set) within the Swift standard library. With COW, Swift does not make a second copy of the data structure until a change is made to that data structure. Therefore, if we pass an array of 50,000 elements to another part of our code, and that code does not actually make any changes to the array, we will avoid the runtime overhead of copying all the elements.

This is a very nice feature and can greatly increase the performance of our applications; however, our custom value types do not automatically get this feature by default. In this section, we will see how we can use reference and value types together, in order to implement the COW feature for our custom value types. To do this, we will create a very basic queue type.

We will start off by creating a backend storage type called BackendQueue and will implement it as a reference type. The following code gives our BackendQueue type the basic functionality for a queue type:

```
fileprivate class BackendQueue<T> {
    private var items = [T]()

    public func addItem(item: T) {
        items.append(item)
    }

    public func getItem() -> T? {
        guard index < items.count else {
            return nil
        }
        return items.remove(at:0)
    }
    public func count() -> Int {
        return items.count
    }
}
```

The BackendQueue type is a generic type that uses an array to store its data. This type contains three methods to add items to the queue, to retrieve items from the queue, and to return the number of items in the queue. We use the fileprivate access level to prevent the use of this type outside of the defining source file because it should only be used to implement the COW feature for our main queue type.

We now need to add a couple of extra items to the BackendQueue type so we can use it to implement the COW feature for the main queue type. The first two things that we will add are a public default initializer and a private initializer that can be used to create a new instance of the BackendQueue type. The following code shows the two initializers:

```
public init() {}
private init(_ items: [T]) {
    self.items = items
}
```

The public initializer will be used to create an instance of BackendQueue with any items in the queue. The private initializer will be used internally to create a copy of itself. Now, we will need to create a method that will use the private initializer to create a copy of itself when needed:

```
public func copy() -> BackendQueue<T> {
    return BackendQueue<T>(items)
}
```

It would be very easy to make the private initializer public, and then let the main queue type call that initializer in order to create the copy; however, it is good practice to keep the logic needed to create the new copy within the type itself. The reason that you should do this is if you need to make changes to the type that may affect how the type is copied, the logic that you need to change is embedded within the type itself and is easy to find. Additionally, if you use BackendQueue as the backend storage for multiple types, you will only need to make the changes to the copy logic in one place.

Here is the final code for the BackendQueue type:

```
fileprivate class BackendQueue<T> {
    private var items = [T]()

    public init() {}
    private init(_ items: [T])   {
        self.items = items
    }

    public func addItem(item: T)   {
        items.append(item)
    }

    public func getItem() -> T? {
        if items.count > 0   {
            return items.remove(at: 0)
        } else {
            return nil
        }
    }
    public func count() -> Int  {
        return items.count
    }
    public func copy() -> BackendQueue<T> {
        return BackendQueue<T>(items)
    }
}
```

Now, let's create our `Queue` type that will use the `BackendQueue` type to implement the COW feature. The following code adds the basic queue functionality to our `Queue` type:

```
struct Queue {
    private var internalQueue = BackendQueue<Int>()

    public mutating func addItem(item: Int) {
        internalQueue.addItem(item: item)
    }
    public mutating func getItem() -> Int? {
        return internalQueue.getItem()
    }
    public func count() -> Int {
        return internalQueue.count()
    }
}
```

The `Queue` type is implemented as a value type. This type has one private property of the `BackendQueue` type, which will be used to store the data. This type contains three methods: to add items to the queue, to retrieve an item from the queue, and to return the number of items in the queue. Now, let's see how we would add the COW feature to the `Queue` type.

Swift has a global function named `isKnownUniquelyReferenced()`. This function will return true if there is only one reference to an instance of a reference type, or false if there is more than one reference.

We will begin by adding a function to check whether there is a unique reference to the `internalQueue` instance. This will be a private function named `checkUniquelyReferencedInternalQueue`. The following code shows how we would implement this method:

```
mutating private func checkUniquelyReferencedInternalQueue() {
    if !isKnownUniquelyReferenced(&internalQueue)   {
        internalQueue = internalQueue.copy()
        print("Making a copy ofinternalQueue")
    } else {
        print("Not making a copy of internalQueue")
    }
}
```

In this method, we check to see whether there are multiple references to the `internalQueue` instances. If there are multiple references, then we know that we have multiple copies of the `Queue` instance, therefore we will create a new copy.

The `Queue` type itself is a value type; therefore, when we pass an instance of the `Queue` type within our code, we are passing a new copy of that instance. The `BackendQueue` type that the `Queue` type is using is a reference type; therefore, when a copy is made of a `Queue` instance, that new copy receives a reference to the original queue's `BackendQueue` instance and not a new copy. This means that each instance of the `Queue` type has a reference to the same `internalQueue` instance. As an example, in the following code, both `queue1` and `queue2` have references to the same `internalQueue` instance:

```
var queue1 = Queue()
var queue2 = queue1
```

Within the `Queue` type, we know that both the `addItem()` and `getItem()` methods change the `internalQueue` instance; therefore, before we make these changes, we will want to call the `checkUniquelyReferencedInternalQueue()` method to create a new copy of the `internalQueue` instance. Let's update these methods in the following code:

```
public mutating func addItem(item: Int) {
    checkUniquelyReferencedInternalQueue()
    internalQueue.addItem(item: item)
}
public mutating func getItem() -> Int? {
    checkUniquelyReferencedInternalQueue();
    return internalQueue.getItem()
}
```

With this code, when either the `addItem()` or `getItem()` methods are called, which will change the data within the `internalQueue` instance. We will use the `checkUniquelyReferencedInternalQueue()` method to create a new instance of the data structure if needed.

Let's add one additional method to the `Queue` type, which will let us see whether there is a unique reference to the `internalQueue` instance or not. Here is the code for this method:

```
mutating public func uniquelyReferenced() -> Bool {
    return isKnownUniquelyReferenced(&internalQueue)
}
```

Here is the full code listing for the `Queue` type:

```swift
struct Queue {
    private var internalQueue = BackendQueue<Int>()

    mutating private func checkUniquelyReferencedInternalQueue() {
        if !isKnownUniquelyReferenced(&internalQueue) {
            print("Making a copy of internalQueue")
            internalQueue = internalQueue.copy()
        } else {
            print("Not making a copy of internalQueue")
        }
    }

    public mutating func addItem(item: Int) {
        checkUniquelyReferencedInternalQueue()
        internalQueue.addItem(item: item)
    }
    public mutating func getItem() -> Int? {
        checkUniquelyReferencedInternalQueue()
        return internalQueue.getItem()
    }
    public func count() -> Int {
        return internalQueue.count()
    }
    mutating public func uniquelyReferenced() -> Bool {
        return isKnownUniquelyReferenced(&internalQueue)
    }
}
```

Now, let's see how the COW functionality works with the `Queue` type. We will start off by creating a new instance of the `Queue` type, adding an item to the queue, and then see if we have a unique reference to the `internalQueue` instance. The following code shows us how to do this:

```swift
var queue3 = Queue()
queue3.addItem(item: 1)

print(queue3.uniquelyReferenced())
```

When we add the item to the queue, the following messages will be printed to the console. This tells us that within the `checkUniquelyReferencedInternalQueue()` method, it was determined that there was only one reference to the `internalQueue` instance:

```
Not making a copy of internalQueue
```

We can verify this by printing the results of the `uniquelyReference()` method into the console. Now, let's make a copy of the `queue3` instance by passing it to a new variable, like this:

```
var queue4 = queue3
```

Now, let's see if we have a unique reference to the `internalQueue` instance of either the `queue3` or `queue4` instance. The following code will do this:

```
print(queue3.uniquelyReferenced())
print(queue4.uniquelyReferenced())
```

This code will print two false messages to the console, letting us know that neither instance has a unique reference to their `internalQueue` instances. Now, let's add an item to either one of the queues. The following code will add another item to the `queue3` instance:

```
queue3.addItem(item: 2)
```

When we add the item to the queue, we will see the following message printed to the console:

```
Making a copy of internalQueue
```

This message tells us that when we added the new item to the queue, a new copy of the `internalQueue` instance was created. To verify this, we can print the results of the `uniquelyReferenced()` methods to the console again. If you do check this, you will see two true messages printed to the console this time, rather than two false messages. We can now add additional items to the queues and we will see that we are not creating new instances of the `internalQueue` instance because each instance of the `Queue` type now has its own copy.

 If you are planning on creating your own data structure that may contain a large number of items, it is recommended that you implement it with the COW feature, as shown here.

Let's see how we would use generics in a protocol-oriented design.

Generics in a protocol-oriented design

Now that we have seen how to use generics, let's see how we can use them in a protocol-oriented design. In a previous example in this chapter, we created a generic `List` type; however, we can greatly improve on this design by using what we have learned throughout this chapter. We will include only a small subset of the actual requirements for a `List` type so we can focus on the design, rather than all the requirements.

With a protocol-oriented design, we always start with the protocol. The following code shows the `List` protocol:

```
protocol List {
    associatedtype T
    subscript<E:  Sequence>(indices: E)   -> [T]
        where E.Iterator.Element == Int { get }
    mutating func add(_  item: T)
    func length() -> Int
    func get(at index: Int) -> T?
    mutating func delete(at index: Int)
}
```

We start the `List` protocol by defining the associated `T` type. This associated type will be the type of data stored in the list. We use the `T` type as the parameter for the `add(item:)` method. We also use the `T` type as the return type for the `get(index:)` method and the subscript. The `add(item:)` method will be used to add an item to the list. The `get(index:)` method and the subscript will be used to retrieve the item(s) at the specified index of the list. The `length()` method will return the number of items in the list, and the `delete(index:)` method will remove an item from the list.

From previous examples in this book, we may think that you would create a protocol extension for the `List` protocol; however, we want to keep our `List` protocol as generic as possible so we can use it for any type of list. We will see how this works as we go through the examples in this section.

Since the `List` types will be data storage structures, let's create a backend storage type that we can use to implement the COW feature for any `List` type that is implemented using a value type. Using the knowledge we learned from the *COW* section of this chapter, we could implement this type like this:

```
private class BackendList<T>  {
    private var items: [T] = []

    public init()  {}
    private init(_ items:  [T])  {
        self.items = items
    }

    public func add(_ item:  T) {
        items.append(item)
    }
    public func length() -> Int {
        return items.count
    }
    public func get(at index: Int) -> T? {
        return items[index]
    }
    public func delete(at index: Int) {
        items.remove(at: index)
    }
    public func copy() -> BackendList<T> {
        return BackendList<T>(items)
    }
}
```

The `BackendList` type implements all the functionality needed to add, get, and delete items from the array that is storing the items for our data structure. We also have methods to get the length of the array and to make a new copy of `BackendList`. All this code should look very familiar at this point.

Now, let's create an `ArrayList` type that will use `BackendList` as the storage mechanism. This code shows us how to create a type that conforms to the `List` protocol and implements the COW feature:

```
struct ArrayList<T>: List {
    private var items = BackendList<T>()

    public subscript<E: Sequence>(indices: E) -> [T]
    where E.Iterator.Element == Int {
        var result = [T]()
        for index in indices  {
```

```
                    if let item = items.get(at:  index) {
                        result.append(item)
                    }
                }
                return result
            }

            public mutating func add(_ item:  T) {
                checkUniquelyReferencedInternalQueue()
                items.add(item)
            }
            public func length() -> Int {
                return items.length()
            }
            public func get(at index: Int) -> T? {
                return items.get(at: index)
            }
            public mutating func delete(at index: Int) {
                checkUniquelyReferencedInternalQueue()
                items.delete(at: index)
            }

            mutating private func checkUniquelyReferencedInternalQueue() {
                if  !isKnownUniquelyReferenced(&items) {
                    print("Making a copy of internalQueue")
                    items = items.copy()
                }   else   {
                        print("Not making a copy of internalQueue")
                }
            }
        }
```

We can create an instance of the ArrayList type and add items, as shown in the following code:

```
var arrayList = ArrayList<Int>()
arrayList.add(1)
arrayList.add(2)
arrayList.add(3)
```

This code will create an instance of the ArrayList type that contains integers and adds three items to it.

Let's look at our design now. The following diagrams show how we designed this data structure:

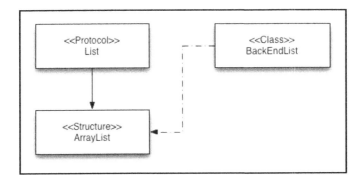

This diagram shows that the `ArrayList` type conforms to the `List` protocol and uses the `BackEndList` type. Now, we can very easily add other types that conform to the `List` protocol, and if they are implemented as a value type, we can also use the same `BackEndList` type to implement the COW feature. The following diagram illustrates this:

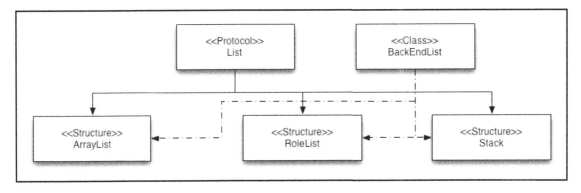

Now that we have seen how to design a basic data structure in a protocol-oriented way with generics, let's look at how generics are used in the Swift standard library.

Generics in the Swift standard library

Generics are used extensively within the Swift standard library and they allow the Swift collection types to store instances of any type. To see this, let's go to http://swiftdoc.org/ and look at the `Array` type. If you click on the **Array** link from the main page, you will see the documentation on the array type. The documentation looks like this:

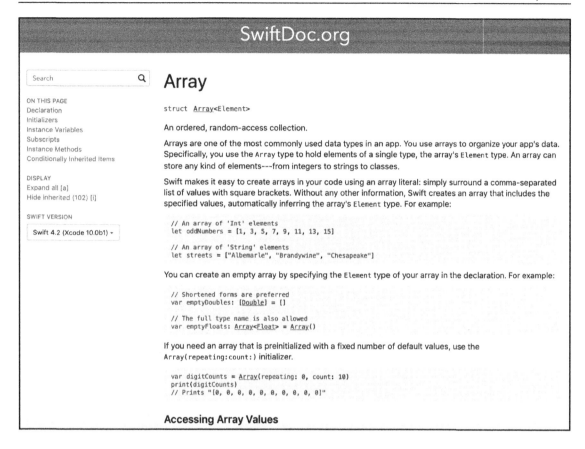

At the top of the page, we see that the array type is defined as `struct Array<Element>`. This tells us that the array type is implemented as a generic value type using a structure. If we now look at the set, we will see that it is also implemented as a generic structure.

Summary

Generics in Swift are extremely powerful. With protocols, we are able to use a common interface to interact with various types that conform to the protocol. Also, when we use generics, we are able to create generic types that can accept instances of any type. When we combine protocols and generics, as we saw with the list types in this chapter, we are able to create very powerful libraries that meet both our present needs and our future needs.

Apple has stated that generics are one of the most powerful features of Swift and that much of the Swift standard library is built using generics. You should keep this in mind as you are writing your applications.

To manage memory within our applications, Swift uses **Automatic Reference Counting (ARC)**. With ARC, for the most part, memory management in Swift simply works. There are instances where ARC requires additional information about relationships to properly manage the memory. In the next chapter, we will look at how ARC works and how to avoid common issues with it.

Memory Management

5

For many years, the primary languages I used were C and C-based object-oriented languages, such as Objective-C and C++. These languages required a good handle on managing memory and knowing when to release memory. Luckily, modern languages such as Swift take care of managing memory for us; however, it is a good idea to understand how memory management works so we can avoid the pitfalls that cause memory management to fail.

In this chapter, we will learn about the following:

- How ARC works
- What a strong reference cycle is
- How to use weak and unowned references

Structures are value types. What this means is that when an instance of a structure is passed within our application, such as a parameter for a method, a new instance of the structure is created in the memory. This new instance of the structure is only valid while the application is in the scope where the structure was created. Once the structure goes out of scope, the new instance of the structure is destroyed, and the memory is released. This makes the memory management of structures pretty easy and somewhat painless.

Classes, on the other hand, are reference types. This means that memory is allocated once when the instance of the class is initially created. When an instance of the class is passed within our application, either as a function argument or by assigning it to a variable, a reference to the original instance is passed. Since the instance of a class may be referenced in multiple scopes (unlike a structure), it cannot be automatically destroyed, and memory is not released when it goes out of scope if it is referenced in another scope.

Therefore, Swift needs some form of memory management to track and release the memory used by instances of classes when the class is no longer needed. To do this, Swift uses **Automatic Reference Counting** (**ARC**) to track and manage memory usage.

With ARC, for the most part, memory management in Swift simply works. ARC will automatically track the references to instances of classes, and when an instance is no longer needed (that is , where there are no references pointing to it), ARC will automatically destroy the instance and release the memory. There are a few instances where ARC requires additional information about relationships to properly manage the memory. Before we look at the instances where ARC needs help, let's look at how ARC works.

How ARC works

Whenever we create a new instance of a class, ARC allocates the memory needed to store that class. This ensures that there is enough memory to store the information associated with that instance of the class, and also locks the memory so that nothing overwrites it. When the instance of the class is no longer needed, ARC will release the memory allocated for the class so that it can be used for other purposes. This ensures that we are not tying up memory that is no longer needed.

If ARC were to release the memory for an instance of a class that was still needed, it would not be possible to retrieve the class information from memory. If we did try to access the instance of the class after the memory was released, there is a possibility that the application would crash. To ensure memory is not released for an instance of a class that is still needed, ARC counts how many times the instance is referenced; that is, how many active properties, variables, or constants are pointing to the instance of the class. Once the reference count for an instance of a class equals zero (nothing is referencing the instance), the memory is marked for release.

All the previous examples run properly in a Playground; however, the following examples will not. When we run the sample code in a Playground, ARC does not release objects that we create; this is by design so that we can see how the application runs as well as the state of the objects at each step. Therefore, we will need to run these samples as an iOS or macOS project. Let's look at an example of how ARC works.

We begin by creating a `MyClass` class with the following code:

```
class MyClass {
    var name = ""
    init(name: String) {
        self.name = name
        print("Initializing class with name \(self.name)")
```

```
    }
    deinit {
        print("Releasing class with name \(self.name)")
    }
}
```

This class contains a property called `name`. It also contains an initializer, which is called when the class is first created, and a deinitializer, which is called just before an instance of the class is destroyed and removed from memory. This deinitializer prints out a message to the console that lets us know that the instance of the class is about to be removed.

Now, let's look at the code that shows how ARC creates and destroys instances of a class:

```
var class1ref1: MyClass? = MyClass(name: "One")
var class2ref1: MyClass? = MyClass(name: "Two")
var class2ref2: MyClass? = class2ref1

print("Setting class1ref1 to nil")
class1ref1 = nil
print("Setting class2ref1 to nil")
class2ref1 = nil
print("Setting class2ref2 to nil")
class2ref2 = nil
```

In the example, we begin by creating two instances of the `MyClass` class named `class1ref1` (which stands for class 1, reference 1) and `class2ref1` (which stands for class 2, reference 1). We then create a second reference to `class2ref1`, named `class2ref2`. Now, in order to see how ARC works, we need to begin setting the references to nil. We start out by setting `class1ref1` to `nil`. Since there is only one reference to `class1ref1`, the deinitializer will be called. Once the deinitializer completes its task, in our case it prints a message to the console letting us know that the instance of the class has been destroyed and the memory has been released.

We then set `class2ref1` to `nil`, but there is a second reference to this class (`class2ref2`), which prevents ARC from destroying the instance so that the deinitializer is not called. Finally, we set `class2ref2` to `nil`, which allows ARC to destroy this instance of the `MyClass` class.

If we run this code, we will see the following output, which illustrates how ARC works:

```
Initializing class with name One
Initializing class with name Two
Setting class1ref1 to nil
Releaseing class with name One
Setting class2ref1 to nil
Setting class2ref2 to nil
Releaseing class with name Two
```

From the example, it seems that ARC handles memory management pretty well. However, it is possible to write code that will prevent ARC from working properly.

Strong reference cycles

A strong reference cycle is where the instances of two classes hold a strong reference to each other, preventing ARC from releasing either instance. Once again, we are not able to use a Playground for this example, so we need to create an Xcode project. In this project, we start off by creating two classes named MyClass1_Strong and MyClass2_Strong with the following code:

```
class MyClass1_Strong {
    var name = ""
    var class2: MyClass2_Strong?
    init(name: String) {
        self.name = name
        print("Initializing class1_Strong with name \(self.name)")
    }
    deinit {
        print("Releasing class1_Strong with name \(self.name)")
    }
}
class MyClass2_Strong {
    var name = ""
    var class1: MyClass1_Strong?
    init(name: String) {
        self.name = name
        print("Initializing class2_Strong with name \(self.name)")
    }
    deinit {
        print("Releasing class2_Strong with name \(self.name)")
    }
}
```

As we can see from the code, `MyClass1_Strong` contains an instance of `MyClass2_Strong`, therefore the instance of `MyClass2_Strong` cannot be released until `MyClass1_Strong` is destroyed. We can also see from the code that `MyClass2_Strong` contains an instance of `MyClass1_Strong`, therefore the instance of `MyClass1_Strong` cannot be released until `MyClass2_Strong` is destroyed. This creates a cycle of dependency in which neither instance can be destroyed until the other one is destroyed. Let's see how this works by running the following code:

```
var class1: MyClass1_Strong? = MyClass1_Strong(name: "Class1_Strong")
var class2: MyClass2_Strong? = MyClass2_Strong(name: "Class2_Strong")

class1?.class2 = class2
class2?.class1 = class1

print("Setting classes to nil")
class2 = nil
class1 = nil
```

In this example, we create instances of both the `MyClass1_Strong` and `MyClass2_Strong` classes. We then set the `class2` property of the `class1` instance to the `MyClass2_Strong` instance. We also set the `class1` property of the `class2` instance to the `MyClass1_Strong` instance. This means that the `MyClass1_Strong` instance cannot be destroyed until the `MyClass2_Strong` instance is destroyed. This means that the reference counters for each instance will never reach zero, therefore ARC cannot destroy the instances, which creates a memory leak. A memory leak is when an application continues to use memory and does not properly release it. This can cause an application to eventually crash.

To resolve a strong reference cycle, we need to prevent one of the classes from keeping a strong hold on the instance of the other class, thereby allowing ARC to destroy them both. When the code is run, you will see output similar to the following:

```
Initializing class1_Strong with name Class1_Strong
Initializing class2_Strong with name Class2_Strong
Setting classes to nil
```

As we can see from the output, neither one of the instances are released. This is because each class contains a strong reference to the other class, therefore neither one can be released. Swift provides two ways to prevent this by letting us define properties as either weak or unowned references.

Unowned references

An unowned reference is a non-strong (or weak) reference to an instance. This means that the reference to the instance is not taken into account by ARC. An unowned reference is always expected to contain a value and should never be nil.

We begin by creating two more classes, MyClass1_Unowned and MyClass2_Unowned:

```
class MyClass1_Unowned {
    var name = ""
    unowned let class2: MyClass2_Unowned
    init(name: String, class2: MyClass2_Unowned) {
        self.name = name
        self.class2 = class2
        print("Initializing class1_Unowned with name \(self.name)")
    }
    deinit {
        print("Releasing class1_Unowned with name \(self.name)")
    }
}
class MyClass2_Unowned {
    var name = ""
    var class1: MyClass1_Unowned?
    init(name: String) {
    self.name = name
        print("Initializing class2_Unowned with name \(self.name)")
    }
    deinit {
        print("Releasing class2_Unowned with name \(self.name)")
    }
}
```

The MyClass1_Unowned class looks pretty similar to classes in the preceding example. The difference here is the MyClass1_Unowned class, where we set the class2 property to unowned, which means it cannot be nil and it does not keep a strong reference to the instance that it is referring to. Since the class2 property cannot be nil, we also need to set it when the class is initialized.

Let's see how we can initialize and deinitialize the instances of these classes with the following code:

```
let class2 = MyClass2_Unowned(name: "Class2_Unowned")
let class1: MyClass1_Unowned? = MyClass1_Unowned(name: "class1_Unowned",
                                                 class2: class2)

class2.class1 = class1

print("Classes going out of scope")
```

In the preceding code, we create an instance of the MyClass2_Unowned class and then use that instance to create an instance of the MyClass1_Unowned class. We then set the class1 property of the MyClass2 instance to the MyClass1_Unowned instance we just created. This creates a reference cycle of dependency between the two classes again, but this time, the MyClass1_Unowned instance doesn't a strong hold on the MyClass2_Unowned instance, allowing ARC to release both instances when they are no longer needed.

If we run this code, we see the following output, showing that both the MyClass3 and MyClass4 instances are released and the memory is freed:

```
Initializing class2_Unowned with name Class2_Unowned
Initializing class1_Unowned with name class1_Unowned
Classes going out of scope
Releasing class2_Unowned with name Class2_Unowned
Releasing class1_Unowned with name class1_Unowned
```

As we can see, both instances are properly released. Once thing to keep in mind when using unowned references is that the instance is deallocated once there are no more strong references to the instance. This means that an instance pointed to by an unowned reference may be deallocated while your application still has an unowned reference to it. This can cause strange behavior or application crashes.

Now let's look at how we would use a weak reference to prevent a strong reference cycle.

Weak references

A weak reference is similar to an unowned reference, where a non-strong (or weak) reference is referencing an instance of a type. The main difference is a weak reference can contain nil. If the instance is deallocated while there is a weak reference referencing it, then the weak reference is set to nil.

Once again, we begin by creating two new classes:

```
class MyClass1_Weak {
    var name = ""
    var class2: MyClass2_Weak?
    init(name: String) {
        self.name = name
        print("Initializing class1_Weak with name \(self.name)")
    }
    deinit {
        print("Releasing class1_Weak with name \(self.name)")
    }
}
class MyClass2_Weak {
    var name = ""
    weak var class1: MyClass1_Weak?
    init(name: String) {
        self.name = name
        print("Initializing class2_Weak with name \(self.name)")
    }
    deinit {
        print("Releasing class2_Weak with name \(self.name)")
    }
}
```

The `MyClass1_Weak` and `MyClass2_Weak` classes look very similar to the previous classes we created, which showed how a strong reference cycle works. The difference is that we define the `class1` property in the `MyClass2_Weak` class as a weak reference.

Now, let's see how we can initialize and deinitialize instances of these classes with the following code:

```
let class1: MyClass1_Weak? = MyClass1_Weak(name: "Class1_Weak")
let class2: MyClass2_Weak? = MyClass2_Weak(name: "Class2_Weak")

class1?.class2 = class2
class2?.class1 = class1

print("Classes going out of scope")
```

In the preceding code, we create instances of the `MyClass1_Weak` and `MyClass2_Weak` classes and then set the properties of those classes to point to the instance of the other class. Once again, this creates a cycle of dependency, but since we set the `class1` property of the `MyClass2_Weak` class to weak, it does not create a strong reference, allowing both instances to be released.

If we run the code, we will see the following output, showing that both the `MyClass5` and `MyClass6` instances are released and the memory is freed:

```
Initializing class1_Weak with name Class1_Weak
Initializing class2_Weak with name Class2_Weak
Classes going out of scope
Releasing class1_Weak with name Class1_Weak
Releasing class2_Weak with name Class2_Weak
```

It is recommended that you avoid creating circular dependencies, as shown in this section, but there are times when you may need them. For those times, remember that ARC needs some help to release them.

Summary

In this chapter, we saw how Swift manages memory using ARC. ARC works so well that we may think that we do not need to worry about memory management, which is exactly why we looked at how ARC can fail with strong reference cycles. We also saw how we can avoid strong reference cycles by using `Weak` or `Unowned` references.

In the next chapter, we will see how Swift can be used as an object-oriented programming language, before seeing how it can be used as a protocol-oriented programming language.

Object-Oriented Programming

6

I was first introduced to object-oriented programming in college when I had a brief introduction to C++. At the time, the C++ programming language was still relatively new. In fact, the first edition of the language was only released three years prior to my introduction to it. The object-oriented programming paradigm was a radical departure from the procedural programming paradigm that I learned in the past and, at the time, it seemed quite overwhelming. Even though I was introduced to object-oriented programming with C++, I really did not do any serious development with it until I learned Java much later. In this chapter, you will learn about the following:

- How Swift can be used as an object-oriented programming language
- How we can develop an API in an object-oriented way
- The benefits of an object-oriented design
- The drawbacks of object-oriented programming

While this book is about protocol-oriented programming, we really need to discuss how Swift can be used as an object-oriented programming language before looking at how it can be used as a protocol-oriented language. Having a good understanding of object-oriented programming will help us understand protocol-oriented programming and give us some insight into the issues it's designed to solve.

What is object-oriented programming?

Object-oriented programming is a design philosophy. Writing applications with an object-oriented programming language is fundamentally different to writing applications with older procedural languages, such as C and Pascal. Procedural languages use a set of instructions to tell the computer what to do step by step, by relying on procedures (or routines). However, object-oriented programming is all about the object. This may seem like a pretty obvious statement given the name, but essentially, when we think about object-oriented programming, we need to think about the object.

The object is a data structure that contains information about the attributes of the object, in the form of properties and the actions performed by, or to, the object in the form of methods. Objects can be considered things and in the English language, they would normally be considered nouns. These objects can be real-world or virtual. If you look around, you will see many real-world objects, and virtually all of them can be modeled in an object-oriented way with attributes and actions.

As I am writing this chapter, I look outside and see numerous trees, grass, my dog, and the fence in our backyard. All of these items can be modeled as objects with both properties and actions.

I am also thinking about one of my all-time favorite energy drinks. That energy drink is Jolt Cola. I'm not sure how many people remember Jolt, but I would not have made it through college without it. A can of Jolt can be modeled as an object with attributes (the volume, quantity of caffeine, temperature, and size) and actions (the act of drinking, and temperature changes).

We could keep the cans of Jolt in a cooler to keep them cold. This cooler could also be modeled as an object because it has attributes (the temperature, the present number cans of Jolt, and a maximum number of cans) and actions (adding and removing cans).

Defining the properties and actions of an object is good, but we also need to understand how the object interacts. For example, when we place a can of Jolt Cola in a cooler that has ice in it, the can will get colder; however, if there isn't any ice in the cooler then the can stays at room temperature. Understanding these interactions is important for designing your objects correctly.

Within a computer application, we cannot create an object without a blueprint that tells the application what properties and actions to expect from the object. In most object-oriented languages, this blueprint comes in the form of a class. A class is a construct that allows us to encapsulate the properties and actions of an object into a single type that models the entity we are trying to represent in our code.

We use initializers within our classes to create instances of the class. We usually use these initializers to set the initial values of the properties for the object, or to perform any other initialization that our class needs. Once we create the instance of a class, we can then use it within our code.

It's important to understand that the class is the backbone of object-oriented programming. Without the class and the object that is created from the class, we would not have object-oriented programming. It is equally important to understand that the class is a reference type, and, unless defined otherwise, can have super- and subclasses.

All of these explanations of object-oriented programming are fine, but nothing demonstrates the concepts better than the actual code. Before we can begin coding, we will need to define some requirements. In this chapter, we will show how we could design vehicle types for a video game in an object-oriented way. In the next chapter, we will then show how we can design the same classes in a protocol-oriented way. Let's see the requirements for the vehicle types.

Requirements for the sample code

When we develop applications, we usually have a set of requirements that we need to work toward. Our sample projects in this chapter and the next are no different. The following is a list of requirements for the vehicle types that we will be creating:

- We will have three categories of vehicles: sea, land, and air. A vehicle can be a member of multiple categories.
- Vehicles may move or attack when they are on a tile that matches any of the categories they are in.
- Vehicles will be unable to move to or attack on a tile that does not match any of the categories they are in.
- When a vehicle's hit points reach zero, the vehicle will be considered incapacitated. We will need to keep all active vehicles in a single array that we can loop through.

For our design in this chapter, we will be demonstrating the design with only a few vehicles, but we know that the number of vehicle types will grow as we develop the game. In this chapter, we will not be implementing a lot of the logic for the vehicles because our focus is on the design and not the code that makes the vehicles move and attack. Let's begin designing our vehicles in an object-oriented way.

Swift as an object-oriented programming language

Swift provides full support for developing applications in an object-oriented way. Prior to Swift 2, Swift was considered to be primarily an object-oriented language in the same way that Java and C# are considered to be object-oriented languages. In this section, we will design the vehicle types in an object-oriented way and look at the advantages and disadvantages of this design.

Class diagrams

Before we look at the code, let's create a very basic class diagram that shows how we would design the vehicle class hierarchy for the object-oriented design. In an object-oriented design, we use class hierarchies to group similarly related classes. Since Swift is a single inheritance language, a class can only have one superclass that it inherits from. The root class in a class hierarchy is the only class without a superclass.

I usually start off by doing a very basic diagram that simply shows the classes themselves without much detail. This helps me picture the class hierarchy in my mind. The following diagram shows the class hierarchy for the object-oriented design:

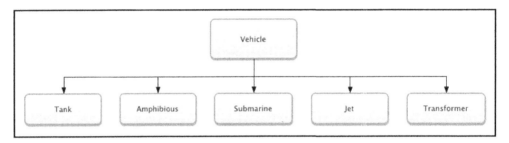

This diagram shows that we have one superclass named Vehicle and five subclasses named Tank, Amphibious, Submarine, Jet, and Transformer. With a class hierarchy, each of the subclasses will inherit all the properties and methods from the superclass; therefore, any common code and properties can be implemented within the Vehicle superclass and all the subclasses will then inherit it.

We may think that, with the three categories (land, air, and sea) in our requirements, we would want to create a larger class hierarchy in which the middle layer would contain separate superclasses for land, air, and sea vehicles. This would allow us to separate the code for each category into its own superclass; however, that is not possible with these requirements because any vehicle type may be a member of multiple categories (land, air, and sea) and with a single inheritance language such as Swift, each class can have one and only one, superclass. For example, this means that if we created separate land and sea superclasses then the Amphibious class could be a subclass of either the land or the sea type, but not both. The following image illustrates this:

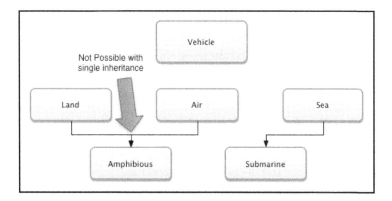

Since Swift is a single-inheritance language and we can have only one superclass for all the vehicle classes, that superclass will need to contain the code required for each of the three categories. Having a single superclass such as this is one of the drawbacks of object-oriented design because the superclass can become very bloated.

Object-oriented design

We will start forming our object-oriented design by creating a `TerrainType` enumeration that will be used to define the different vehicle, attack, and movement types. The `TerrainType` enumeration is defined as follows:

```
enum TerrainType {
    case land
    case sea
    case air
}
```

Vehicle superclass

Now let's see how we would define the `Vehicle` superclass and the properties within this:

```
class Vehicle {
    fileprivate var vehicleTypes = [TerrainType]()
    fileprivate var vehicleAttackTypes = [TerrainType]()
    fileprivate var vehicleMovementTypes = [TerrainType]()
    fileprivate var landAttackRange = -1
    fileprivate var seaAttackRange= -1
    fileprivate var airAttackRange= -1
    fileprivate var hitPoints = 0
}
```

We start the `Vehicle` type off by defining seven properties. The first three properties are arrays of the `TerrainType` type. These three arrays will keep track of vehicle type (the `vehicleTypes` array), types of terrain the vehicle can attack from (the `vehicleAttackTypes` array), and types of terrain the vehicle can move to (the `vehicleMovementTypes` array).

The next three properties (`landAttackRange`, `seaAttackRange`, and `airAttackRange`) will contain the attack range of the vehicle for each of the different terrain types. If the attack range is less than zero, we assume that it cannot do that type of attack. Finally, the last property will keep track of the hit points of the vehicle.

The preference for each of these properties, except for the `hitPoints` property, is to be constants; however, a subclass cannot set/change the value of a constant defined in a superclass. This means that we will need to rely on Swift's access control functionality to control access to these properties.

We defined the properties as `fileprivate` variables because we need to set them apart from the subclasses; however, we do not want external entities to change them. This access control was introduced in Swift 3 and allows access to the properties and methods from any code within the same source file that the item is defined in. For this to work, the subclass needs to be defined in the same physical file as the superclass, which is definitely not the ideal solution because this file could get very large. However, in this object-oriented design, it is the best option we have to prevent these properties from being changed by instances of other types. If we find that we have more than a handful of vehicle types, we would probably change the access control to internal so we could put the implementation of the vehicles in separate files.

Since the properties are marked as `fileprivate`, we will need to create some better methods to retrieve the values of the properties. We will also create methods to see what types of terrain the vehicle can attack from and move to. Let's see these methods in the following example:

```swift
func isVehicleType(type: TerrainType) -> Bool {
    return vehicleTypes.contains(type)
}
func canVehicleAttack(type: TerrainType) -> Bool {
    return  vehicleAttackTypes.contains(type)
}
func canVehicleMove(type:  TerrainType) -> Bool {
    return vehicleMovementTypes.contains(type)
}
func doLandAttack() {}
func doLandMovement() {}
```

```
func doSeaAttack() {}
func doSeaMovement() {}

func doAirAttack() {}
func doAirMovement() {}

func takeHit(amount: Int) { hitPoints -= amount }
func hitPointsRemaining() ->Int { return  hitPoints }
func isAlive() -> Bool { return hitPoints > 0 ? true : false }
```

The `isVehicleType` method accepts one parameter of the `TerrainType` type and it will return true if the `vehicleTypes` array contains that terrain type. This will allow the external code to see if the vehicle is of a certain type. The next two methods also accept a parameter of the `TerrainType` type and will return true if the `vehicleAttackTypes` or `vehicleMovementTypes` arrays contain that terrain type. These two methods would be used to see whether a vehicle can move to, or attack from, a certain type of terrain.

The next six methods define the attacks on, or movement from, different terrains for the vehicle. The next two methods will be used to deduct hit points when the vehicle takes a hit and returns the remaining hit points. The final method will be used to determine whether the vehicle is still alive or not. There are a couple of issues we can see right away with this design. Let's take a quick look at these before we move on.

One big issue relating to this design, as we noted earlier, is that if we want to use the file-private access control that will prevent direct access to the properties, then all the subclasses need to be in the same physical file as the `Vehicle` superclass. Given how large the vehicle classes can be, we probably don't want them all in the same source file. To avoid this, we could set the property's access controls to internal, but that wouldn't prevent the properties from being changed by instances of other types. This is a major drawback of object-oriented design because we don't want external types to have direct access to the properties.

Another issue of the object-oriented design is that we need to provide methods that will allow the vehicle to attack from and move through each of the different terrain types, even though most vehicles will not be able to attack from and move through all the different terrains. Even though there is no code in the method implementations, the external code will still be able to call any of the attack and movement methods. For example, even though our `Submarine` type is a sea-only type, external code will be able to call the movement and attack methods for land and air types.

Superclasses that are bloated, such as this one, are a major issue in single-inheritance, object-oriented programming languages such as Swift. With bloated superclasses such as our `Vehicle` type, it is very easy to make a mistake, or give a some type functionality it should not have, or deny a functionality it should have. For example, it would be very easy to set the `airAttackRange` property for the `Submarine` type giving it the ability to attack from the air, which a submarine obviously cannot do.

 In this example, we are only defining a very small subset of the functionality that would be needed for our vehicle types in a video game. Imagine how big the `Vehicle` superclass could be if all the functionality was being implemented.

Vehicle subclasses

Let's look at how we would subclass the `Vehicle` class by creating the `Tank`, `Amphibious`, and `Transformer` classes. We will start with the `Tank` class:

```
class Tank: Vehicle {
    override init() {
        super.init()
        vehicleTypes = [.land]

        vehicleAttackTypes = [.land]
        vehicleMovementTypes = [.land]
        landAttackRange = 5
        hitPoints = 68
    }
    override func doLandAttack() {
        print("Tank Attack")
    }
    override func doLandMovement() {
        print("Tank Move")
    }
}
```

The `Tank` class is a subclass of the `Vehicle` class, and we begin this class by overriding the default initializer. In the initializer, we set several inherited properties. Notice that we add the land value to the `vehicleTypes`, `vehicleAttackTypes`, and `vehicleMovementTypes` arrays. This specifies that the `Tank` type is a land vehicle and can attack from and move to land tiles.

Using arrays to keep track of the type of vehicle the class is related to and the types of terrain the vehicle can move to and attack from is another issue of this object-oriented design. Even for the most experienced developer, it is very easy to enter the wrong value into the arrays, causing unexpected behavior.

In the `Tank` class, we also override the `doLandAttack()` and `doLandMovement()` methods from the `Vehicle` superclass since the `Tank` class is a land vehicle. We do not override the other attack and movement methods from the `Vehicle` superclass because the `Tank` should not be moving to or attacking from the sea or air terrains. Even though we do not override these methods, they are still a part of the `Tank` class because they are inherited from the `Vehicle` superclass, and there is no way to prevent the external code from calling these methods.

Now let's look at the `Amphibious` and `Transformer` classes. These classes are very similar to the `Tank` class, except that they can move through, and attack from, multiple terrain types. We will look at the `Amphibious` class first. This class can move to and attack from both land and sea terrains, as shown in the following example:

```
class Amphibious: Vehicle {
    override init() {
        super.init()
        vehicleTypes = [.land, .sea]
        vehicleAttackTypes = [.land, .sea]
        vehicleMovementTypes = [.land, .sea]

        landAttackRange = 1
        seaAttackRange = 1

        hitPoints = 25
    }
    override func doLandAttack() {
        print("Amphibious Land Attack")
    }
    override func doLandMovement() {
        print("Amphibious Land Move")
    }
    override func doSeaAttack() {
        print("Amphibious Sea Attack")
    }
    override func doSeaMovement() {
        print("Amphibious Sea Move")
    }
}
```

The Amphibious class is very similar to the Tank class that we have just seen. The difference between the two types is that the Tank type was defined as a land-only unit, while the amphibious type is defined as both a land and sea unit. Since it is a land and sea unit, we override the land attack and movement methods, as well as the sea attack and movement methods. We also add both the sea and land values to the vehicleTypes, vehicleAttackTypes, and vehicleMovementTypes arrays.

Now let's see the Transformer class. This type will have the ability to move and attack from all three terrain types, as shown in the following code example:

```
class  Transformer:  Vehicle  {
    override  init()  {
        super.init()
        vehicleTypes = [.land, .sea, .air]
        vehicleAttackTypes = [.land, .sea, .air]
        vehicleMovementTypes  =  [.land,  .sea,  .air]

        landAttackRange=7
        seaAttackRange=10
        airAttackRange  =  12
        hitPoints  =  75
    }

    override  func  doLandAttack()  {
        print("Transformer  Land  Attack")
    }
    override  func  doLandMovement()  {
        print("Transformer  Land  Move")
    }
    override  func  doSeaAttack()  {
        print("Transformer  Sea  Attack")
    }
    override  func  doSeaMovement()  {
        print("Transformer  Sea  Move")
    }
    override  func  doAirAttack()  {
        print("Transformer  Air  Attack")
    }
    override  func  doAirMovement()  {
        print("Transformer  Air  Move")
    }
}
```

For the `Transformer` type, we override all three movement and attack methods from the `Vehicle` superclass since the `Transformer` has the ability to move and attack from all three terrain types. We also added all three terrain types to the vehicle types, `vehicleAttackTypes`, and `vehicleMovementTypes` arrays.

Now that we have created the vehicle types, let's see how they would be used. One of the original requirements was to be able to keep instances of all the vehicle types in a single array. This will give us the ability to loop through all active vehicles and perform any actions needed. For this, we will use polymorphism.

Polymorphism

Polymorphism comes from the Greek words *poly* (meaning many) and *morph* (meaning forms). In computer science, we use polymorphism when we want to use a single interface to represent multiple types within our code. Polymorphism gives us the ability to interact with multiple types in a uniform manner. With object-oriented programming languages, we can achieve polymorphism through subclassing, where we interact with the various subclasses using the interface provided by the superclass.

Let's see how we would use polymorphism to keep all instances of the various vehicle types in a single array and interact with them. Since all the vehicle types are subclasses of the `Vehicle` superclass, we can create an array of vehicle types, and store instances of any type that is a subclass of the `Vehicle` superclass, as shown here:

```
var vehicles = [Vehicle]()

varvh1=Amphibious()
varvh2=Amphibious()
var vh3 = Tank()
var vh4 = Transformer()

vehicles.append(vh1)
vehicles.append(vh2)
vehicles.append(vh3)
vehicles.append(vh4)
```

Now we can loop through and interact with each instance using the interface presented by the `Vehicle` type. The following code illustrates this:

```
for (index, vehicle) in vehicles.enumerated() {
    if vehicle.isVehicleType(type: .air) {
        print("Vehicle at \(index) is Air")
        if vehicle.canVehicleAttack(type: .air) {
            vehicle.doAirAttack()
```

```
        }
        if vehicle.canVehicleMove(type: .air) {
           vehicle.doAirMovement()
        }
     }
   if vehicle.isVehicleType(type: .land) {
       print("Vehicle at \(index)  is  Land")
       if  vehicle.canVehicleAttack(type: .land) {
         vehicle.doLandAttack()
       }
       if vehicle.canVehicleMove(type: .land) {
           vehicle.doLandMovement()
       }
   }
   if vehicle.isVehicleType(type: .sea) {
       print("Vehicle at \(index) is Sea")
       if vehicle.canVehicleAttack(type: .sea) {
         vehicle.doSeaAttack()
       }
       if vehicle.canVehicleMove(type: .sea) {
           vehicle.doSeaMovement()
       }
   }
  }
}
```

In this code, we loop through the vehicles array and use the `isVehicleType(type:)` method to determine whether the vehicle is of a certain type and then call the appropriate movement and attack methods. Note that we do not use an `if-else` or a `switch` statement here, because any vehicle may be a member of multiple types and we want to recheck the type, even if the vehicle matched a previous type.

If we wanted to filter the results to only return instances of the `Vehicle` types that were air units, we could use the `where` clause with the `for` loop. The following code illustrates this:

```
for (index, vehicle) in vehicles.enumerated() where
vehicle.isVehicleType(type: .air) {
    if vehicle.isVehicleType(type: .air)  {
        print("**Vehicle at \(index) is Air")
        if vehicle.canVehicleAttack(type: .air) {
           vehicle.doAirAttack()
        }
        if vehicle.canVehicleMove(type: .air) {
           vehicle.doAirMovement()
        }
    }
}
```

This code would only perform the attack and movement methods if the isVehicleType(type:) method returned true for the air type.

This design works well enough, but as we will see in Chapter 7, *Protocol-Oriented Programming*, with Swift, we can resolve a lot of the issues presented here with a protocol-oriented design. Let's review the drawbacks of object-oriented design so we can see how protocol-oriented programming addresses them in the next chapter.

Issues with object-oriented design

Two of the issues that we saw with the object-oriented design were directly related to each other and are the result of Swift being a single-inheritance language. Remember a single-inheritance language is a language that limits a class to having not more than one superclass.

Object-oriented design with a single-inheritance language, such as Swift, can lead to bloated superclasses because we may need to include functionality that is needed by only a few of the subclasses. This leads to the second issue related to Swift being a single-inheritance language, which is the inheritance of functionality that a type does not need.

In our design, we had to include the functionality for all three terrain types because the vehicle types may be able to move or attack in any of the terrain types. This extra functionality may lead to errors in our code if we're not careful. It's really easy to accidentally create a class like this:

```swift
class Infantry: Vehicle {
    override init() {
        super.init()
        vehicleTypes      = [.land]
        vehicleAttackTypes    = [.land]
        vehicleMovementTypes  = [.sea]

        landAttackRange = 1
        seaAttackRange  = 1

        hitPoints   =  25
    }
    override func doLandAttack() {
        print("Amphibious  Land  Attack")
    }
    override func doLandMovement() {
        print("Amphibious  Land  Move")
    }
}
```

Looking at this code, we can easily see that the `vehicleMovementTypes` array contains the `sea` type rather than the `land` type, but it is also easy to make mistakes like this.

Another issue in object-oriented design is that we cannot create constants in our superclass that can be set by the subclasses. In our design, there were several properties that we would like to set in the initializer of our subclasses and then never change. It would be ideal if we could make these constant; however, a constant defined in one class cannot be set in a subclass of that type.

The last issue that we saw was the inability to set a property or method to be accessible only by subclasses of that type. To get around this, we used the `fileprivate` access control to say that only code defined in the same source file could access the properties; however, this workaround is not an ideal solution because we may not want to put all the subclasses in the same source file as the superclass. If we did put the subclasses in a separate file, then we would have to set the access controls to internal; however, this would not prevent other types within the project from modifying them.

Summary

In this chapter, we saw how we could design vehicles for a video game in an object-oriented way. We also saw how we could use polymorphism with a class hierarchy. There were several issues with this object-oriented design and most of these drawbacks were directly related to Swift being a single-inheritance language.

In the next chapter, we will look at how we can design the same vehicle types in a protocol-oriented way to see how it addresses the issues we saw with the object-oriented design.

Protocol-Oriented Programming

7

This book is about protocol-oriented programming. When Apple announced Swift 2 at the **World Wide Developers Conference (WWDC)** in 2015, they also declared that Swift was the world's first protocol-oriented programming language. From its name, we may assume that protocol-oriented programming is all about the protocol; however, this would be a wrong assumption to make. Protocol-oriented programming is about so much more than just the protocol; it is actually a new way of not only writing applications, but also how we think about programming.

In this chapter, we will cover the following topics:

- What protocol-oriented programming is
- How we can use protocol composition
- How we can use protocol inheritance
- How protocol-oriented programming compares to object-oriented programming

In `Chapter 6`, *Object-Oriented Programming,* we explored how we could design vehicle types in an object-oriented way. In this chapter, we will design the same vehicle types in a protocol-oriented way and compare the two designs.

After some of the more advanced topics that were discussed in previous chapters, the examples in this chapter may seem a little basic; that is, almost a step back. This was done on purpose. The examples in this chapter are written to help you begin thinking in a protocol-oriented way and to help your mind break free of the object-oriented way of thinking that you are probably used to. Once you do that, you can begin incorporating some of the more advanced topics that we have previously covered.

The designs that we present in this chapter will demonstrate the basics of a protocol-oriented design and are written to help you to begin thinking in a protocol-oriented way. You should not forget about some of the more advanced features that we covered earlier in this book, such as generics.

Let's start off by reviewing the requirements for our vehicle types.

Requirements for the sample code

When we develop applications, we usually have a set of requirements that we need to work toward. Our sample projects in this chapter and the next are no different. The following is a list of requirements for the vehicle types that we will be creating:

- We will have three categories of vehicles: sea, land, and air. A vehicle can be a member of multiple categories.
- Vehicles may move or attack when they are on a tile that matches any of the categories they are in.
- Vehicles will be unable to move to or attack on a tile that does not match any of the categories they are in.
- When a vehicle's hit points reach zero, then the vehicle will be considered incapacitated. Therefore, we will need to keep all the active vehicles in a single array that we can loop through.

In this chapter, we will be demonstrating our design with only a few vehicles, but we know that the number of vehicle types will grow as we develop the game. In this chapter, we will not be implementing a lot of the logic for the vehicles because our focus is on the design, not the code that makes the vehicles move and attack.

So, let's now take a look at how we can design the vehicles in a protocol-oriented way.

Swift as a protocol-oriented programming language

Just as we did with the object-oriented design, we will start off by creating a very basic diagram that demonstrates how to design the vehicle types in a protocol-oriented way. Just like the object-oriented diagram, this will be a very basic diagram that simply shows the types themselves without much detail:

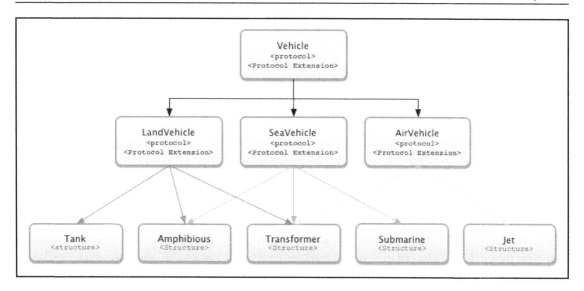

The protocol-oriented design is relatively different from the object-oriented design. In the object-oriented design, we started the design with the superclass, which became the focus of the design and all the subclasses inherited functionality and properties from that superclass.

In the protocol-oriented design, we start the design with the protocol. The protocols and protocol extensions are the focus of the protocol-oriented design; however, as we have seen throughout this book, protocol-oriented design isn't simply about the protocol.

In this new design, we use three techniques that make protocol-oriented programming significantly different from object-oriented programming. These techniques are protocol inheritance, protocol composition, and protocol extensions. Let's start off by looking at protocol inheritance.

Protocol inheritance

Protocol inheritance is where one protocol can inherit requirements from other protocols. This is quite similar to class inheritance in object-oriented programming; however, instead of inheriting functionality from a superclass, we are inheriting requirements from the protocol. One advantage that protocol inheritance has over class inheritance, in Swift, is that protocols can inherit the requirements from multiple protocols. In our example, the LandVehicle, SeaVehicle, and AirVehicle protocols inherit the requirements from the Vehicle protocol.

It is also important to note that, with a combination of protocol extensions and protocols, we do have the ability to inherit functionality. Now, let's take a look at protocol composition.

Protocol composition

Protocol composition allows types to conform to more than one protocol. In our example, there are some types (such as the `Tank`, `Submarine`, and `Jet` structures) that conform to a single protocol; however, there are also two types (the `Amphibious` and `Transformer` structures) that take advantage of protocol composition by conforming to multiple protocols.

Protocol inheritance and composition are extremely important to protocol-oriented design because they allow us to create smaller and more specific protocols. This allows us to avoid the bloated superclasses that we saw with the object-oriented designs. We do need to be careful not to create protocols that are too granular because they will become hard to maintain and manage. Now, let's take a look at protocol extensions.

Protocol extensions

Protocol extensions allow us to extend a protocol to provide methods and property implementations to conforming types. This gives us the ability to provide common implementations to all the conforming types, eliminating the need to provide an implementation for each individual type or the need to create a class hierarchy. While protocol extensions may not seem too exciting, once you understand how powerful they are, they will transform the way you think about application design.

The Vehicle protocol

Let's begin the implementation by creating the `Vehicle` protocol. The `Vehicle` protocol, for this example, will define a single property named `hitPoints` that will keep track of the vehicle's remaining hit points:

```
protocol Vehicle {
    var hitPoints: Int {get set}
}
```

If you recall from our object-oriented design, we had three methods defined in the superclass that all vehicle types used. These methods were `takeHit(amount:)`, `hitPointsRemaining()`, and `isAlive()`. The implementations of these methods will be the same for every vehicle type; therefore, they are great candidates to be implemented with protocol extensions.

One thing to note is that the properties defined in a protocol cannot be private. The reason for this is that protocols are used to define the methods, properties, and other requirements that the confirmed class will expose to other entities. A private property isn't exposed to other entities.

The following code demonstrates how we can create a `Vehicle` protocol extension, and how we can implement these three methods within the extension:

```
extension Vehicle {
    mutating func takeHit(amount: Int) {
        hitPoints -= amount
    }
    func hitPointsRemaining() -> Int {
        return hitPoints
    }
    func isAlive() -> Bool {
        return hitPoints > 0 ? true : false
    }
}
```

Now, any type that conforms to the `Vehicle` protocol, or any type that conforms to a protocol that inherits from the `Vehicle` protocol, will automatically receive these methods. Protocols that inherit requirements from another protocol also inherit the functionality provided by the protocol's extensions.

Now, let's take a look at how we can define the `LandVehicle`, `SeaVehicle`, and `AirVehicle` protocols:

```
protocol LandVehicle: Vehicle {
    var landAttack: Bool {get}
    var landMovement: Bool {get}
    var landAttackRange: Int {get}
    func doLandAttack()
    func doLandMovement()
}

protocol SeaVehicle: Vehicle {
    var seaAttack: Bool {get}
    var seaMovement: Bool {get}
    var seaAttackRange: Int {get}
```

```
        func doSeaAttack()
        func doSeaMovement()
    }

    protocol AirVehicle: Vehicle {
        var airAttack: Bool {get}
        var airMovement: Bool {get}
        var airAttackRange: Int {get}
        func doAirAttack()
        func doAirMovement()
    }
```

There are a couple of things to note about these protocols. The first thing is that they all inherit the requirements from the Vehicle protocol, which also means they inherit the functionality from the Vehicle protocol extension.

Another thing to note about these protocols is that they only contain the requirements needed for their particular vehicle types. If you recall, the Vehicle superclass from the object-oriented design contained the requirements for all vehicle types. Dividing the requirements up into three separate protocols makes the code much safer, easier to maintain, and easier to manage. If we do need some common functionality, we can add a protocol extension to any or all of the protocols.

We defined the properties for these protocols with only the get attribute, which means we will be defining the properties as constants within the types that conform to these protocols. This is a really big advantage of using the protocol-oriented design because it prevents external code from changing the values once they are set, which could introduce errors that are hard to trace.

Vehicle implementations

Now, let's take a look at how to create types that conform to these protocols. We will create the same Tank, Amphibious, and Transformer types that we implemented in the object-oriented design. Let's start with the Tank type, as follows:

```
    struct Tank: LandVehicle {
        var hitPoints = 68
        let landAttackRange = 5
        let landAttack = true
        let landMovement = true
        func doLandAttack() { print("Tank Attack") }
        func doLandMovement() { print("Tank Move") }
    }
```

There are several differences between the `Tank` type defined here and the `Tank` type defined in the object-oriented design. To see these differences, let's examine the `Tank` type that was defined in the object-oriented design:

```
class Tank: Vehicle {
    override init() {
        super.init() vehicleTypes = [.land]
        vehicleAttackTypes = [.land]
        vehicleMovementTypes = [.land]
        landAttackRange = 5
        hitPoints = 68
    }
    override func doLandAttack() { print("Tank  Attack") }
    override func doLandMovement() { print("Tank  Move") }
}
```

The first thing that we can see is that the `Tank` type from our object-oriented design is a class, which is a reference type, while the `Tank` type designed in a protocol-oriented way is a structure, which is a value type. Protocol-oriented design does not tell us that we must use value types, but it does say that they are preferred. This means that we could define the `Tank` type as a class in both paradigms and it may be preferable to do so depending on the overall design of our application.

One of the main reasons to choose value types over reference types is safety; if we always get a unique copy of the value type instances, then we can trust that no other parts of our code can change that instance. This is especially helpful within a multithreaded environment, where we would not want another thread to change the data while we are using it because this can create bugs that are very hard to replicate and track. In our case, we will probably need the ability to allow one part of our code to make a change to the vehicle instances and have that change persisted. While this is not the normal behavior of a value type, we can use an `inout` parameter to achieve this. We will demonstrate how to do this later on in this chapter.

Another difference between the two `Tank` types is that the one designed in a protocol-oriented way can use the default initializer that the structure provides, and we are able to define the properties as constants. Since the properties are constants, they can't be changed once they are set. On the other hand, in the `Tank` type from the object-oriented design, we had to override the initializer and then set the properties within the initializer. The properties in the object-oriented design were defined as variables, which allows them to be changed after they are set.

One thing that we do not see when we look at the two `Tank` types is that the `Tank` type from the protocol-oriented design contains only the functionality for land vehicles. The `Tank` type from the object-oriented design inherits the functionality and properties for both the sea and air types as well as the land type, even though it does not need that functionality.

Now, let's take a look at how we can create the `Amphibious` type:

```
struct Amphibious: LandVehicle, SeaVehicle {
    var hitPoints = 25
    let landAttackRange = 1
    let seaAttackRange = 1
    let landAttack = true
    let landMovement = true
    let seaAttack = true
    let seaMovement = true
    func doLandAttack() {
        print("Amphibious Land Attack")
    }
    func doLandMovement() {
        print("Amphibious Land Move")
    }
    func doSeaAttack() {
        print("Amphibious Sea Attack")
    }
    func doSeaMovement() {
        print("Amphibious Sea Move")
    }
}
```

The `Amphibious` type is very similar to the `Tank` type; however, it uses protocol composition to conform to multiple vehicle types. This allows it to have the functionality of both the land and sea types. Now, let's see how we can implement the `Transformer` type:

```
struct Transformer: LandVehicle, SeaVehicle, AirVehicle {
    var hitPoints = 75
    let landAttackRange = 7
    let seaAttackRange = 5
    let airAttackRange = 6
    let landAttack = true
    let landMovement = true
    let seaAttack = true
    let seaMovement = true
    let airAttack = true
    let airMovement = true
    func doLandAttack() {
        print("Transformer Land Attack")
    }
    func doLandMovement() {
        print("Transformer Land Move")
    }
    func doSeaAttack() {
        print("Transformer Sea Attack")
    }
    func doSeaMovement() {
        print("Transformer Sea Move")
    }
    func doAirAttack() {
        print("Transformer Sea Attack")
    }
    func doAirMovement() {
        print("Transformer Sea Move")
    }
}
```

Since the `Transformer` type can move to and attack from all three terrain types, we use protocol composition to have it conform to the `LandVehicle`, `SeaVehicle`, and `AirVehicle` protocols.

Let's take a look at how we can use these new types. As with our object-oriented design, we have the requirement to be able to keep instances of all the vehicle types in a single array. This enables us to loop through all the active vehicles and perform any actions needed. For this, we will use polymorphism just as we did with our object-oriented design; however, with the protocol-oriented design, we will use the interface provided by the protocols to interact with the instances of the vehicle types. Let's demonstrate how to do this by creating an array and putting several instances of the vehicle types into it:

```
var vehicles = [Vehicle]()

var vh1 = Amphibious()
var vh2 = Amphibious()
var vh3 = Tank()
var vh4 = Transformer()

vehicles.append(vh1)
vehicles.append(vh2)
vehicles.append(vh3)
vehicles.append(vh4)
```

This code looks exactly like the code from our object-oriented design. In this code, we create an array that will store instances of types that conform to the Vehicle type. With protocol inheritance, this means the array will also accept types that conform to protocols that inherit the Vehicle protocol. In our example, this means that the array will accept instances of types that conform to the LandVehicle, SeaVehicle, AirVehicle, and Vehicle protocols.

The array, in this example, is defined to contain instances of types that conform to the Vehicle protocol. This means that we can use the interface defined by the Vehicle protocol to interact with the types in the array. Looking at the Vehicle protocol, we can see that this really is not very useful; however, we can attempt to typecast the instance to see whether they conform to a particular protocol. The following code illustrates this:

```
for (index, vehicle) in vehicles.enumerated() {
    if let Vehicle = vehicle as? AirVehicle {
        print("Vehicle at \(index) is Air")
    }
    if let Vehicle = vehicle as? LandVehicle {
        print("Vehicle at \(index) is Land")
    }
    if let Vehicle = vehicle as? SeaVehicle {
        print("Vehicle at \(index) is Sea")
    }
}
```

In the preceding code, we use a `for` loop statement to loop through the vehicles array. We use an `as?` typecast operator to check whether the instances conform to one of the protocols (such as the `AirVehicle`, `LandVehicle`, and `SeaVehicle` protocols), and, if so, we print out a message.

Accessing the vehicle types in this manner is very similar to how we accessed them in the object-oriented example; however, what if we only wanted to get one type of vehicle rather than all the vehicles? Well, we can do this with the `where` clause. The following example shows how to do this:

```
for (index, vehicle) in vehicles.enumerated() where vehicle is LandVehicle
{
    let vh = vehicle as! LandVehicle
    if vh.landAttack {
        vh.doLandAttack()
    }
    if vh.landMovement {
        vh.doLandMovement()
    }
}
```

In this example, we use the `where` keyword to filter the results of the `for` loop to retrieve only instances that conform to the `LandVehicle` protocol. We can then typecast any instance that is returned from the `for` loop as an instance that conforms to the `LandVehicle` protocol and interact with it using the interface provided by the protocol.

Now that we have finished redesigning, let's summarize how protocol-oriented programming differs from object-oriented programming.

Summarizing protocol-oriented programming and object-oriented programming

In this chapter and `Chapter 6`, *Object-Oriented Programming* before it, we learned how Swift can be used as both an object-oriented programming language and a protocol-oriented programming language. In these chapters, we discovered that there are two major differences between the two designs.

The first major difference is that with a protocol-oriented design, we should start with the protocol rather than a superclass. We can then use protocol extensions to add functionality to the types that conform to that protocol, or types that conform to protocols that inherit from that protocol. With object-oriented programming, we started with a superclass. When we designed our vehicle types in a protocol-oriented way, we converted the `Vehicle` superclass from the object-oriented design, to a `Vehicle` protocol, and then used a protocol extension to add the common functionality needed.

In the protocol-oriented example, we used protocol inheritance and protocol composition in order to create protocols with very specific requirements. This allowed us to create concrete types that only contained the functionality needed for that type. In the object-oriented design, the concrete types inherited all the functionality provided by the `Vehicle` superclass.

The second big difference is the use of value types (structures) rather than reference types (classes) for our vehicle types. Apple's documentation states that developers should prefer value types over reference types where appropriate. In our example, we used structures that are value types; however, we could have used reference types. We will discuss this difference in more detail later on in this chapter.

Both the object-oriented design and the protocol-oriented design used polymorphism to let us interact with different types using a single interface. With the object-oriented design, we used the interface provided by the superclass to interact with all the subclasses. In the protocol-oriented design, we used the interface provided by the protocols and the protocol extensions to interact with the types that conform to the protocols.

Now that we have summarized the differences between object-oriented design and protocol-oriented design, let's take a closer look at these differences.

Differences between object-oriented programming and protocol-oriented programming

I mentioned, at the beginning of this chapter, that protocol-oriented programming is about so much more than just the protocol, and that it is a new way of not only writing applications, but also thinking about programming. In this section, we will examine the differences between our two designs in order to understand what that statement really means.

As developers, our primary goal is to always develop an application that works properly, but we should also be focused on writing clean and safe code. Clean code is code that is very easy to read and understand. It is important to write clean code because any code that we write will need to be maintained by someone, and that someone is usually the person who wrote it. There is nothing worse than looking back at the code you wrote and not being able to understand what it does. It is also a lot easier to find errors in code that is clean and easy to understand.

By safe code, we mean code that is hard to break. There is nothing more frustrating for us developers than making a small change in our code and then have errors pop up throughout the code base. By writing clean code, our code will be inherently safer because other developers will be able to look at the code and understand exactly what it does.

Now, let's compare protocol and protocol extensions to superclasses.

Protocol and protocol extensions compared with superclasses

In the object-oriented programming example, we created a `Vehicle` superclass from which all the vehicle classes were derived. In the protocol-oriented programming example, we used a combination of protocols and protocol extensions to achieve the same result; however, there are several advantages to the protocol-oriented design.

To refresh our memory of the two solutions, let's examine the code for both the `Vehicle` superclass and the `Vehicle` protocol and protocol extension. The following code shows the `Vehicle` superclass:

```
class Vehicle {
    fileprivate var vehicleTypes = [TerrainType]()
    fileprivate var vehicleAttackTypes = [TerrainType]()
    fileprivate var vehicleMovementTypes = [TerrainType]()

    fileprivate var landAttackRange = -1
    fileprivate var seaAttackRange = -1
    fileprivate var airAttackRange = -1

    fileprivate var hitPoints = 0

    func isVehicleType(type: TerrainType) -> Bool {
        return vehicleTypes.contains(type)
    }
    func canVehicleAttack(type: TerrainType) -> Bool {
```

```
        return vehicleAttackTypes.contains(type)
    }
    func canVehicleMove(type: TerrainType) -> Bool {
        return vehicleMovementTypes.contains(type)
    }
    func doLandAttack() {}
    func doLandMovement() {}
    func doSeaAttack() {}
    func doSeaMovement() {}
    func doAirAttack() {}
    func doAirMovement() {}
    func takeHit(amount:  Int) { hitPoints -= amount }
    func hitPointsRemaining() -> Int { return hitPoints }
    func isAlive() -> Bool { return hitPoints > 0 ? true : false }
}
```

The `Vehicle` superclass is a complete type that we can create instances of. This can be a good thing or a bad thing. There are times, such as with this example, when we should not be creating instances of the superclass. For this, we can still use protocols with object-oriented programming, however; we will need to use protocol extensions to add the common functionality, and that leads us down the protocol-oriented programming path.

Now, let's see how we used protocols and protocol extensions in the protocol-oriented design. We will start off by looking at the `Vehicle` protocol and the `Vehicle` protocol extension:

```
protocol Vehicle {
    var hitPoints: Int {get set}
}
extension Vehicle {
    mutating functakeHit(amount: Int) {
        hitPoints -= amount
    }
    func hitPointsRemaining() ->Int {
        return hitPoints
    }
    func isAlive() -> Bool {
        returnhitPoints > 0 ? true: false
    }
}
```

We then created three additional protocols, one for each type of vehicle, and used protocol inheritance to inherit the requirements and functionality from the `Vehicle` protocol. The following are the `LandVehicle`, `SeaVehicle`, and `AirVehicle` protocols:

```
protocol LandVehicle: Vehicl e{
    var landAttack: Bool {get}
    var landMovement: Bool{get}
    var landAttackRange: Int {get}

    func doLandAttack()
    func doLandMovement()
}

protocol SeaVehicle: Vehicle {
    var seaAttack: Bool {get}
    var seaMovement: Bool {get}
    var seaAttackRange: Int {get}

    func doSeaAttack()
    func doSeaMovement()
}

protocol AirVehicle: Vehicle {
    var airAttack: Bool {get}
    var airMovement: Bool {get}
    var airAttackRange: Int {get}

    func doAirAttack()
    func doAirMovement()
}
```

The code in both solutions is pretty safe and easy to understand; however, the protocol-oriented design is safer. By separating the implementation from the definition and dividing the requirements into small, more specific protocols, we are able to eliminate the need for a bloated superclass, and also prevent types from inheriting functionality they do not need.

There are three clear advantages that protocols/protocol extensions have in our design. The first advantage is that types can conform to multiple protocols. This means that we can create numerous protocols that contain very specific functionality, rather than creating a single monolithic superclass. We can see this in our example where the `Vehicle` superclass contained the functionality for land, sea, and air vehicles while, in the protocol-oriented design, we were able to create three protocols, one for each type of vehicle.

The second advantage that protocol/protocol extensions have is that we can use protocol extensions to add functionality without needing the original code. This means that we can extend any protocol, even the protocols that are a part of the Swift language itself. To add functionality to our superclass, we need to have the original code, otherwise, we need to subclass the type; however, this will create a new type. We could use extensions to add functionality to a superclass; however, in general, we use extensions to add functionality to a specific class rather than adding functionality to a class hierarchy. In Chapter 3, *Extensions,* we learned why we should use caution when using extensions to add functionality to a class hierarchy.

The third advantage that protocols/protocol extensions have is that protocols can be adopted by classes, structures, and enumerations, while class hierarchies are restricted to class types. Protocols/protocol extensions give us the option to use value types where appropriate.

Implementing vehicle types

The implementations of vehicle types were slightly different between the object-oriented example and the protocol-oriented example; however, the difference is still pretty significant. We will look at the differences between these two examples, but first, let's take a look at the code again to remind us how we implemented the vehicle types. We will look at how we implemented the Tank type in the object-oriented example first:

```
class Tank: Vehicle {
    override init() {
        super.init() vehicleTypes = [.land]
        vehicleAttackTypes = [.land]
        vehicleMovementTypes = [.land]
        landAttackRange = 5

        hitPoints = 68
    }
    override func doLandAttack() {
        print("Tank Attack")
    }
    override func doLandMovement() {
        print("Tank Move")
    }
}
```

This class is a subclass of the Vehicle superclass, and it implements a single initializer. While this is a pretty simple and straightforward implementation, we really need to fully understand what the superclass expects in order to implement the type properly. For example, if we do not fully understand the Vehicle superclass, we may forget to set the landAttackRange property. In our example, forgetting to set this property will cause the instances of the Tank type to be unable to attack properly.

Now, let's take a look at how we implemented a vehicle type in the protocol-oriented programming example:

```
struct Tank: LandVehicle {
    var hitPoints = 68
    let landAttackRange = 5
    let landAttack = true
    let landMovement = true

    func doLandAttack() { print("Tank Attack") }
    func doLandMovement() { print("Tank Move") }
}
```

The Tank type from the protocol-oriented design conforms to the LandVehicle protocol and uses the default initializer provided by the structure. We can say that the protocol-oriented design is a lot safer and easier to understand because of the way properties and initializers are implemented in both of these examples.

In the object-oriented programming example, all the properties are defined in the superclass as variables. We will need to look at the code or the documentation for the superclass to see what properties are defined and how they are defined. If we forget to set something in a subclass, the compiler will happily compile the application and not warn us.

With protocols, we also need to look at the protocol itself, or the documentation for the protocol, in order to see which properties to implement. The difference is that if we forget to implement any of the requirements, then the compiler will warn us and refuse to compile until we properly set everything. We also have the ability to define any of the properties as constants, whereas with the object-oriented design, we had to define them as variables.

Using value and reference types

In this chapter, we implemented the vehicle types as structures, which are value types. We also mentioned that it may be preferable to implement these types as reference types. The reason we say this is that the instance of the vehicle types represent a single vehicle in our game and any time something happens to that instance, such as taking damage from another vehicle, we would like that change to be persisted.

When we pass an instance of a value type to another part of our code, we are passing a copy of that instance and not the instance itself. This can cause problems when we want to persist changes that are applied to our types. Let's look at this problem with some code. We will start off by creating a function that will apply damage to a vehicle type when it is implemented as a reference type, just like we did with the object-oriented design:

```
func takeHit(vehicle: Vehicle) {
    vehicle.takeHit(amount: 10)
}
```

We can then use this function like this:

```
var vh = Tank()
takeHit(vehicle: vh)
print(vh.hitPointsRemaining())
```

This works as expected and, at the end of the code, the `vh` instance of the `Tank` type will have 58 hit points remaining. This code will not work for value types. Even if the Swift compiler would let us do this, the vehicle instance in the `takeHit(vehicle:)` method is a copy of the `vh` instance that we passed in; therefore, any changes made to the vehicle instance would not persist back to the original `vh` instance. There are lots of times that we want this behavior, but there are also times, such as with our vehicle types, that we want the changes to persist. We can replicate the behavior of reference types with value types, but it does take a little more code. The following function demonstrates how we could create a function that accepts an instance of a value type and persists any changes made to the original instance:

```
func takeHit<T: Vehicle>(vehicle: inout  T) {
    vehicle.takeHit(amount: 10)
}
```

This function is defined as a generic function that has one parameter that conforms to the `Vehicle` protocol. The parameter is also marked as an `inout` parameter, which means that any changes made to that parameter, within the function, are persisted back to the original instance.

We would then use this function like this:

```
var tank = Tank()
takeHit(vehicle: &tank)
print(tank.hitPointsRemaining())
```

When we call this function, we need to put an ampersand (&) before the instance of the `Vehicle` type, which means we are passing a reference to the instance and not the value. This means that any changes you make within the function will be persisted back to the original `Vehicle` instance.

So, which programming paradigm is better? Let's find out.

The winner is...

As we were reading through this chapter, and examining the advantages that protocol-oriented programming has over object-oriented programming, we may think that protocol-oriented programming is clearly superior to object-oriented programming. However, that assumption may not be totally accurate.

Object-oriented programming has been around since the 1970s, and is a battle-tested programming paradigm. Protocol-oriented programming is the new kid on the block, and was designed to correct some of the issues with object-oriented programming. I have personally used the protocol-oriented programming paradigm in a couple of projects and I am very excited about its possibilities.

Object-oriented programming and protocol-oriented programming have similar philosophies, such as creating custom types that can model real-world or virtual objects. They both use polymorphism to use a single interface to interact with multiple types. The difference is in how we design the application.

In my opinion, the code base in a project that uses protocol-oriented programming is much safer and easier to read compared to a project that uses object-oriented programming. This does not mean that I am going to abandon object-oriented programming altogether. I can still see plenty of need for class hierarchy and inheritance.

Remember, when we are designing our application, we should always use the right tool for the right job. We would not want to use a chainsaw to cut a piece of 2 x 4 timber, but we also would not want to use a circular saw to cut down a tree. Therefore, the winner is the developer, as we have the choice of using different programming paradigms, rather than being limited to only one.

Summary

In this chapter, we learned how to design vehicles for a video game in a protocol-oriented way. We discovered how we could use protocol composition and protocol inheritance, which allowed us to create smaller and more specific protocols instead of using a single superclass. We also examined how protocol-oriented programming resolved some of the issues that we encountered with the object-oriented design.

In the next chapter, we will look at how we can implement some of the more popular design patterns with Swift.

8
Adopting Design Patterns in Swift

While the first publication of the Gang of Four's *Design Patterns: Elements of Reusable Object-Oriented Software* was released in October 1994, so far in this book, I have only been paying attention to design patterns over the last 10 to 12 years. Like most experienced developers, when I first started reading about design patterns, I recognized a lot of the patterns because I had already been using them without realizing what they were. Over the past 10 years or so, I do not believe I have written a serious application without using at least one of the Gang of Four's design patterns. I will tell you that I am definitely not a design pattern zealot, and if I get into a conversation about design patterns, there are usually only a couple of them that I can name without having to look them up. But the things that I do remember are the concepts and philosophies behind the major patterns and the problems they are designed to solve. This way, when I encounter one of these problems, I can look up the appropriate pattern and apply it. So, remember as you go through this chapter, to take the time to understand the concepts behind the design patterns rather than trying to memorize the patterns themselves.

In this chapter, you will learn about the following topics:

- What design patterns are
- What types of patterns make up the creational, structural, and behavioral categories of design patterns
- How to implement the builder, factory method, and singleton creational patterns in Swift
- How to implement the bridge, facade, and proxy structural patterns in Swift
- How to implement the strategy, command, and observer behavioral patterns in Swift

What are design patterns?

Every experienced developer has a set of informal strategies that shapes how they design and write applications. These strategies are themselves shaped by the developer's past experiences and the obstacles that they have had to overcome in previous projects. While these developers might swear by their own strategies, this does not mean that their strategies have been fully vetted. The use of these strategies can also introduce inconsistent implementations between different projects and developers.

While the concept of design patterns dates back to the mid-80s, they did not gain popularity until the Gang of Four released their book *Design Patterns: Elements of Reusable Object-Oriented Software*, published in 1994. The book's authors, Erich Gamma, Richard Helm, Ralph Johnson, and John Vlissides discuss the pitfalls of object-oriented programming and describe 23 classic software design patterns. These 23 patterns are broken up into three categories: creational, structural, and behavioral.

A design pattern identifies a common software development problem and provides a strategy to deal with it. These strategies have been proven, over the years, to be an effective solution for the problems they are intended to solve. Using these patterns can greatly speed up the development process because they provide solutions that have already been proven to solve several common software development problems.

Another advantage that we get when we use design patterns is consistent code that is easy to maintain, because months or years from now, when we look at our code, we will recognize the patterns and understand what the code does. If we properly document our code and document the design pattern we are implementing, it will also help other developers understand what our code is doing.

The two main philosophies behind design patterns are code reusability and flexibility. As a software architect, it is essential that we build reusability and flexibility into our code. This allows us to easily maintain our code in the future and makes it easier for our applications to expand to meet future requirements, because we all know how quickly requirements change.

While there is a lot to like about design patterns, and they are extremely beneficial for developers and architects, they are not the solution for world hunger that some developers make them out to be. At some time in your development career, you will probably meet a developer or an architect who thinks that design patterns are immutable laws. These developers usually try to force the use of design patterns even when they are not necessary. A good rule of thumb is to make sure that you have a problem that needs to be fixed before you try to fix it.

Design patterns are starting points for avoiding and solving common programming problems. We can think of each design pattern as a recipe for a food dish. Just like a good recipe, we can tinker and adjust it to meet our particular tastes, but we usually do not want to stray too far from the original recipe because we may mess it up.

There are also times when we do not have a recipe for a certain dish that we want to make, just like there are times when there isn't a design pattern to solve the problem we face. In cases such as these, we can use our knowledge of design patterns and their underlying philosophy to come up with an effective solution for our problem.

Design patterns are split into the following three categories:

- **Creational patterns:** Creational patterns support the creation of objects
- **Structural patterns:** Structural patterns deal with types and object compositions
- **Behavioral patterns:** Behavioral patterns communicate between types

While the Gang of Four defined over 20 design patterns, we are only going to look at examples of some of the more popular patterns in this chapter. Let's start off by looking at creational patterns.

> Design patterns were originally defined for object-oriented programming. In this chapter, we will focus on implementing the patterns in a more protocol-oriented way where possible. For this reason, the examples in this chapter may look a little different from the examples in other design pattern books, but the underlying philosophy of the solutions will be the same.

Creational patterns

Creational patterns are design patterns that deal with how an object is created. There are two basic ideas behind creational patterns. The first is the encapsulation of the knowledge of which concrete types should be created, and the second involves hiding how instances of these types are created.

There are five well-known patterns that are a part of the creational pattern category. They are as follows:

- **Abstract factory pattern:** This provides an interface for creating related objects without specifying the concrete type
- **Builder pattern:** This separates the construction of a complex object from its representation so that the same process can be used to create similar types

- **Factory method pattern:** This creates objects without exposing the underlying logic of how the object (or the type of object) is created
- **Prototype pattern:** This creates an object by cloning an existing one
- **Singleton pattern:** This allows one (and only one) instance of a class for the lifetime of an application

In this chapter, we are going to show examples of how to implement the singleton, builder, and factory method patterns in Swift. Let's start off by looking at one of the most controversial and possibly overused design patterns, the singleton pattern.

The singleton design pattern

The use of the singleton pattern is a fairly controversial subject among certain corners of the development community. One of the main reasons for this is that the singleton pattern is probably the most misused pattern of them all. Another reason that this pattern is controversial is that the singleton pattern introduces a global state into an application, which provides the ability to change the object at any point within the application. The singleton pattern can also introduce hidden dependencies and tight compiling. My personal opinion is that if the singleton pattern is used correctly, there is nothing wrong with using it; however, we do need to be careful not to misuse it.

The singleton pattern restricts the instantiation of a class to a single instance for the lifetime of an application. This pattern is very effective when we need exactly one instance to coordinate actions within our application. An example of a good use of a singleton is if our application communicates with a remote device over Bluetooth and we also want to maintain that connection throughout our application. Some would say that we could pass the instance of the connection class from one page to the next, which is essentially what a singleton is. In my opinion, the singleton pattern, in this instance, is a much cleaner solution, because with the singleton pattern, any page that needs the connection can get it without forcing every page to maintain the instance. This also allows us to maintain the connection without having to reconnect each time we go to another page.

Understanding the problem

The problem the singleton pattern is designed to address is when we need one, and only one, instance of a type for the lifetime of our application. The singleton pattern is usually used when we need centralized management of an internal or external resource and a single global point of access. Another popular use of the singleton pattern is when we want to consolidate a set of related activities, needed throughout our application, that does not maintain a state.

In Chapter 3, *Extensions*, we used the singleton pattern for our text validation types because we wanted to create a single instance of the types that could then be used by all the components of the application without requiring us to create new instances of the types. These text validation types did not have a state that could be changed; they only had methods that performed the validation on the text and constants that defined how to validate the text. While some may disagree with me, I believe types such as these are excellent candidates for the singleton pattern because there is no reason to create multiple instances of these types.

Understanding the solution

There are several ways to implement the singleton pattern in Swift. The way that is presented here uses class constants that were first introduced in version 1.2 of Swift. With this method, a single instance of the class is created the first time we access the class constant. We will then use the class constant to gain access to this instance throughout the lifetime of our application. We will also create a private initializer that will prevent external code from creating additional instances of the class.

 Note that we use the word "class" in this description and not "type". The reason for this is that the singleton pattern can only be implemented with reference types.

Implementing the singleton pattern

Let's look at how we implement the singleton pattern with Swift. The following code example shows how to create a singleton class:

```
class MySingleton {
    static let sharedInstance = MySingleton()
    var number = 0
    private init() {}
}
```

Within the MySingleton class, we create a static constant named sharedInstance that contains an instance of the MySingleton class. A static constant such as this can be called without having to instantiate the class. Since we declared the sharedInstance constant static, only one instance will exist throughout the life cycle of the application, thereby creating the singleton pattern. We also created the private initiator that will prevent external code from creating another instance of the MySingleton class.

Now, let's see how this pattern works. The `MySingleton` pattern has another property called number, which is of the Integer type. We will monitor how this property changes as we use the `sharedInstance` property to create multiple variables of the `MySingleton` type, as shown in the following code:

```
var singleA = MySingleton.sharedInstance
var singleB = MySingleton.sharedInstance
var singleC = MySingleton.sharedInstance
singleB.number = 2
print(singleA.number)
print(singleB.number)
print(singleC.number)
singleC.number = 3
print(singleA.number)
print(singleB.number)
print(singleC.number)
```

In this example, the `sharedInstance` property was used to create three variables of the `MySingleton` type. The number property was initially set to the number 2 using the second `MySingleton` instance (`singleB`). When the value of the number property for `singleA`, `singleB`, and `singleC` was printed to the console, we saw that all three equaled the number 2. Then, the value of the number property was changed to the number 3 using the third `MySingleton` instance (`singleC`). Now, when the value of the number property for all three instances is printed to the console, all three instances' properties have the value of 3. This example verifies the fact that all three instances of the `MySingleton` type point to the same instance because when the value of the number property in any of the instances changes, the values of all three instances change.

In this example, the singleton pattern was implemented using a reference (class) type because we wanted to ensure that only one instance of the type existed throughout the application. If this pattern was implemented with a value type, such as a structure or an enumeration, we would run the risk of having multiple instances of this type. If you recall, each time an instance of a value type is passed, the code is actually passing a copy of that instance. This means that if the singleton pattern was implemented with a value type, then each time an instance of the type was passed to another part of the code, that code would receive a new copy of the instance, thereby breaking this pattern.

The singleton pattern can be very useful when the state of an object must be maintained throughout the life cycle of the application; however, we should be careful not to overuse it. The singleton pattern should not be used unless there is a specific requirement for having one, and only one, instance of a class throughout the life cycle of the application. If the singleton pattern is used simply for convenience, then it is probably being misused.

Keep in mind that while Apple recommends that we prefer value types to reference types, there are still plenty of examples, such as the singleton pattern, where a reference type is needed. When we continuously tell ourselves to prefer value types to reference types, it can be very easy to forget that there are times where a reference type is needed. Don't forget to use reference types with this pattern.

Now, let's look at the builder design pattern.

The builder design pattern

The builder pattern helps with the creation of complex objects and enforces the process of how these objects are created. This pattern is generally used to separate the creation logic from the complex type and put it in another type. This will be the same construction process used to create different representations of the type.

Understanding the problem

The problem that the builder pattern is designed to address is when an instance of a type requires numerous configurable values. The configuration options could be set when an instance of the type is created, but that can cause issues if the options are not set correctly or the proper values for all the options are unknown. Another issue is the amount of code that may be needed to set all the configurable options each time an instance is created.

Understanding the solution

The builder pattern solves this problem by introducing an intermediary known as a **builder** type. This builder type contains most, if not all, of the information necessary to create an instance of the original complex type.

There are two methods that can be used to implement the builder pattern. The first method is to have multiple builder types where each of the builder types contains the information to configure the original complex type in a specific way. The second method implements the builder pattern with a single builder type that sets all of the configurable options to a default value that can then be changed as needed.

In this section, we will look at both ways to use the builder pattern because it is important to understand how each works.

Implementing the builder pattern

Let's start off by looking at how to create a complex structure without the builder pattern to see the problem that the builder pattern is designed to solve.

The following code creates a structure named `BurgerOld` and does not use the builder pattern:

```
truct BurgerOld {
    var name: String
    var patties: Int
    var bacon: Bool
    var cheese: Bool
    var pickles: Bool
    var ketchup: Bool
    var mustard: Bool
    var lettuce: Bool
    var tomato: Bool
    init(name: String, patties: Int, bacon: Bool, cheese: Bool, pickles:
    Bool, ketchup: Bool, mustard: Bool, lettuce: Bool, tomato: Bool) {
        self.name = name
        self.patties = patties
        self.bacon = bacon
        self.cheese = cheese
        self.pickles = pickles
        self.ketchup = ketchup
        self.mustard = mustard
        self.lettuce = lettuce
        self.tomato = tomato
    }
}
```

In the `BurgerOld` structure, there are several properties that define which condiments are on the burger and the name of the burger. These properties must be known when an instance of the `BurgerOld` structure is created, and so the initializer requires us to define each item.

This can lead to some complex initializations throughout the application, not to mention that if there was more than one standard burger type (bacon cheeseburger, cheeseburger, hamburger, and so on), then we would need to make sure that each is defined correctly. Let's see how we can create instances of the `BurgerOld` class:

```
// Create Hamburger
var burgerOld = BurgerOld(name: "Hamburger", patties: 1, bacon: false,
                          cheese: false, pickles: false, ketchup: false,
                          mustard: false, lettuce: false, tomato: false)

// Create Cheeseburger
var cheeseburgerOld = BurgerOld(name: "Cheeseburger", patties: 1,
                               bacon: false, cheese: false, pickles:
                               false, ketchup: false, mustard:
                               false, lettuce: false, tomato: false)
```

Creating instances of the `BurgerOld` type in this manner requires a lot of code. Now, let's see how we can improve the creation of these types by using the builder pattern. This example will use multiple builder types where each builder type will define the condiments that are on a particular type of burger. Let's start by creating a `BurgerBuilder` protocol that will have the following code in it:

```
protocol BurgerBuilder {
    var name: String {get}
    var patties: Int {get}
    var bacon: Bool {get}
    var cheese: Bool {get}
    var pickles: Bool {get}
    var ketchup: Bool {get}
    var mustard: Bool {get}
    var lettuce: Bool {get}
    var tomato: Bool {get}
}
```

This protocol simply defines the nine properties that will be required for any type that implements this protocol. Now, let's create two structures that implement this protocol, the `HamburgerBuilder` and the `CheeseBurgerBuilder` structures:

```
struct HamburgerBuilder: BurgerBuilder {
    let name = "Burger"
    let patties = 1
    let bacon = false
    let cheese = false
    let pickles = true
    let ketchup = true
    let mustard = true
    let lettuce = false
```

```
        let tomato = false
    }

    struct CheeseBurgerBuilder: BurgerBuilder {
        let name = "CheeseBurger"
        let patties = 1
        let bacon = false
        let cheese = true
        let pickles = true
        let ketchup = true
        let mustard = true
        let lettuce = false
        let tomato = false
    }
```

The `HamburgerBuilder` and `CheeseBurgerBuilder` structures simply define the values for each of the required properties. In more complex types, we might need to initialize additional resources.

Now, let's look at the `Burger` structure, which will use instances of the `BurgerBuilder` protocol to create instances of itself. The following code shows this new `Burger` type:

```
    struct Burger {
        var name: String
        var patties: Int
        var bacon: Bool
        var cheese: Bool
        var pickles: Bool
        var ketchup: Bool
        var mustard: Bool
        var lettuce: Bool
        var tomato: Bool
        init(builder: BurgerBuilder) {
            self.name = builder.name
            self.patties = builder.patties
            self.bacon = builder.bacon
            self.cheese = builder.cheese
            self.pickles = builder.pickles
            self.ketchup = builder.ketchup
            self.mustard = builder.mustard
            self.lettuce = builder.lettuce
            self.tomato = builder.tomato
        }
        func showBurger() {
            print("Name:\(name)")
            print("Patties: \(patties)")
            print("Bacon:\(bacon)")
            print("Cheese:\(cheese)")
```

```
        print("Pickles: \(pickles)")
        print("Ketchup: \(ketchup)")
        print("Mustard: \(mustard)")
        print("Lettuce: \(lettuce)")
        print("Tomato:\(tomato)")
    }
}
```

In the previous `BurgerOld` structure, the initializer took nine arguments, one for each constant defined in the structure. In the new Burger structure, the initializer takes one argument, which is an instance of a type that conforms to the `BurgerBuilder` protocol. This new initializer allows us to create instances of the Burger class as follows:

```
// Create Hamburger
var myBurger = Burger(builder: HamburgerBuilder())
myBurger.showBurger()

// Create Cheeseburger with tomatos
var myCheeseBurgerBuilder = CheeseBurgerBuilder()
var myCheeseBurger = Burger(builder: myCheeseBurgerBuilder)

// Let's hold the tomatos
myCheeseBurger.tomato = false
myCheeseBurger.showBurger()
```

If we compare how instances of the new `Burger` structure are created to the earlier `BurgerOld` structure, it is pretty clear that it is easier to create instances of this new `Burger` structure. We also know that we are correctly setting the property values for each type of burger because the values are set directly in the builder classes.

There is a second method that can be used to implement the builder pattern. Rather than having multiple builder types, there can be a single builder type that sets all the configurable options to default values. The values can then be changed as needed. I use this implementation method a lot when I am updating older code because it is easy to integrate it with pre-existing code.

For this implementation, a single `BurgerBuilder` structure is created. This `BurgerBuilder` structure will be used to create instances of the `BurgerOld` structure and will, by default, set all the ingredients to their default values. There will also be several methods in the `BurgerBuilder` structure that can be used to change the default values prior to creating an instance of the `BurgerOld` structure. The following code shows this new `BurgerBuilder` type:

```
struct BurgerBuilder1 {
    var name = "Burger"
```

```
        var patties = 1
        var bacon = false
        var cheese = false
        var pickles = true
        var ketchup = true
        var mustard = true
        var lettuce = false
        var tomato = false
        mutating func setPatties(choice: Int) {self.patties = choice}
        mutating func setBacon(choice: Bool) {self.bacon = choice}
        mutating func setCheese(choice: Bool) {self.cheese = choice}
        mutating func setPickles(choice: Bool) {self.pickles = choice}
        mutating func setKetchup(choice: Bool) {self.ketchup = choice}
        mutating func setMustard(choice: Bool) {self.mustard = choice}
        mutating func setLettuce(choice: Bool) {self.lettuce = choice}
        mutating func setTomato(choice: Bool) {self.tomato = choice}
        func buildBurgerOld(name: String) -> BurgerOld {
            return BurgerOld(name: name, patties: self.patties,
                           bacon: self.bacon, cheese: self.cheese,
                           pickles: self.pickles, ketchup: self.ketchup,
                           mustard: self.mustard, lettuce: self.lettuce,
                           tomato: self.tomato)
        }
    }
```

In the `BurgerBuilder` structure, the nine properties (ingredients) are defined for the burger. There is also a setter method for each of the properties, except for the name property. We also create one method named `buildBurgerOld()` that will create an instance of the `BurgerOld` structure based on the values of the properties for the `BurgerBuilder` instance. The `BurgerBuilder` structure can be used as follows:

```
var burgerBuilder = BurgerBuilder1()
burgerBuilder.setCheese(choice: true)
burgerBuilder.setBacon(choice: true)
var jonBurger = burgerBuilder.buildBurgerOld(name: "Jon's Burger")
```

In this example, an instance of the `BurgerBuilder` structure is created. The `setCheese()` and `setBacon()` methods are used to add cheese and bacon to the burger. Finally, the `buildBurgerOld()` method is called to create the instance of the Burger structure.

Both of these methods that are used to implement the builder pattern greatly simplify the creation of the complex type. Both methods also ensure that the instances are properly configured with default values. If you find yourself creating instances of types with very long and complex initialization commands, I would recommend that you look at the builder pattern to see whether you can use it to simplify the initialization.

For our final example of a creational pattern, we will look at the factory method pattern.

The factory method pattern

The factory method pattern uses methods to create instances of objects without specifying the exact type that will be created. This allows the code to pick the appropriate type to create at runtime.

I find that the factory pattern is one of the patterns that I use a lot. It is also one of the patterns that developers tend to recognize when they first start reading about design patterns because they have used it in previous projects.

Understanding the problem

The problem that the factory pattern is designed to solve is when there are multiple types that conform to a single protocol and the appropriate type to instantiate needs to be chosen at runtime.

Understanding the solution

The factory method pattern encapsulates the logic that is used to select the type to instantiate within a single method. This method exposes only the protocol (or base class) to the code that calls it and does not reveal the details of how a particular type was selected.

Implementing the factory method pattern

To demonstrate how to use the factory method pattern, we will use the text validation types that were created in `Chapter 3`, *Extensions*. In this example, a function will be created that will determine the text validation type to use based on the parameters passed into the factory method by the code that called it.

As a refresher, the code for the `TextValidation` protocol and the `TextValidation` protocol extension are shown in the following code:

```
protocol TextValidation {
    var regExFindMatchString: String {get}
    var validationMessage: String {get}
}

extension TextValidation {
    var regExMatchingString: String {
        get {
            return regExFindMatchString + "$"
        }
    }
    func validateString(str: String) -> Bool {
        if let _ = str.range(of: regExMatchingString,
                             options: .regularExpression) {
            return true
        } else {
            return false
        }
    }
    func getMatchingString(str: String) -> String? {
        if let newMatch = str.range(of: regExFindMatchString,
                                   options: .regularExpression) {
            return String(str[newMatch])
        } else {
            return nil
        }
    }
}
```

Two properties are defined within the `TextValidation` protocol named `regExFindMatchString` and `validationMessage`. Within the protocol extension, one computed property is implemented named `regExMatchingString` and two methods named `validateString()` and `getMatchingString()` are implemented.

Now, three types that conform to the `TextValidation` protocol are created, as shown in the following code:

```
class AlphaValidation: TextValidation {
    static let sharedInstance = AlphaValidation()
    private init(){}
    let regExFindMatchString = "^[a-zA-Z]{0,10}"
    let validationMessage = "Can only contain Alpha characters"
}
```

```
class AlphaNumericValidation: TextValidation {
    static let sharedInstance = AlphaNumericValidation()
    private init(){}
    let regExFindMatchString = "^[a-zA-Z0-9]{0,10}"
    let validationMessage = "Can only contain Alpha Numeric characters"
}

class NumericValidation: TextValidation {
    static let sharedInstance = NumericValidation()
    private init(){}
    let regExFindMatchString = "^[0-9]{0,10}"
    let validationMessage = "Display Name can contain a maximum of
                             15 Alphanumeric Characters"
}
```

The `AlphaValidation` class can be used to validate strings to ensure that they contain a maximum of 10 alphabetical characters. The `NumericValidation` class can be used to validate strings to ensure that they contain a maximum of 10 numeric characters. Finally, the `AlphaNumericValidation` class can be used to validate strings to ensure that they contain a maximum of 10 alphanumeric characters.

To use these validation classes, there needs to be a way to determine which class to use to validate a string value. The factory method pattern can help with this determination, and can be implemented as shown:

```
func getValidator(alphaCharacters: Bool, numericCharacters: Bool) ->
TextValidation? {
    if alphaCharacters && numericCharacters {
        return AlphaNumericValidation.sharedInstance
    } else if alphaCharacters && !numericCharacters {
        return AlphaValidation.sharedInstance
    } else if !alphaCharacters && numericCharacters {
        return NumericValidation.sharedInstance
    } else {
        return nil
    }
}
```

The `getValidator()` method accepts two parameters, both of the Boolean type, named `alphaCharacters` and `numericCharacters`. These parameters define the type of validation needed. An optional type whose value conforms to the `TextValidation` protocol is returned based on the values of the parameters.

One of the biggest advantages of using this pattern is that all the logic regarding how the text validation types are selected is encapsulated in this one function. This means that if the logic used to select the text validation type changes, the only code that needs to change is the code in that function, and we will not need to refactor the entire code base. As an example, if we wish to replace the `AlphaValidation` class with a new `AlphaSpacesValidation` class, the only code that needs to change is within this function.

To do this, we would use the `getValidator()` method, as shown in the following code:

```
var str = "abc123"
var validator1 = getValidator(alphaCharacters: true,
                              numericCharacters: false)
print("String validated: \(validator1?.validateString(str: str))")

var validator2 = getValidator(alphaCharacters: true,
                              numericCharacters: true)
print("String validated: \(validator2?.validateString(str: str))")
```

In this code, the `validator1` variable contains an instance of the `AlphaValidation` type. When the `validateString()` method is called for this instance, it returns a false value because the `str` variable contains numeric values. The `validator2` variable contains an instance of the `AlphaNumericValidation` type. When the `validateString()` method is called for this instance, it returns true because the validation class looks for both alpha and numeric characters.

One of the key ideas behind creational patterns is that we take the logic regarding how and what to create out of our general code base and put it into specific types or functions. Then, when we need to make changes to our code in the future, the logic is encapsulated in a single spot and can be easily changed, rather than being spread throughout our code.

Now, let's look at structural design patterns.

Structural design patterns

Structural design patterns describe how types can be combined to form larger structures. These larger structures can generally be easier to work with, and hide a lot of the complexity of the individual types. Most patterns in the structural pattern category involve connections between objects.

There are seven well-known patterns that are part of the structural design pattern type. These are as follows:

- **Adapter**: This allows types with incompatible interfaces to work together
- **Bridge:** This is used to separate the abstract elements of a type from the implementation, so the two can vary
- **Composite**: This allows us to treat a group of objects as a single object
- **Decorator:** This lets us add or override behavior in an existing method of an object
- **Facade**: This provides a simplified interface for a larger and more complex body of code
- **Flyweight**: This allows us to reduce the resources needed to create and use a large number of similar objects
- **Proxy**: This is a type that acts as an interface for another class or classes

In this chapter, we are going to look at some examples of how to use the bridge, facade, and proxy patterns in Swift. Let's start off by looking at the bridge pattern.

The bridge pattern

The bridge pattern decouples the abstraction from the implementation so that they can both vary independently. The bridge pattern can also be thought of as a two-layer abstraction.

Understanding the problem

The bridge pattern is designed to solve a couple of problems, but the one we are going to focus on here tends to arise over time as new requirements come in with new features. At some point, as these new requirements and features come in, there will be a need to change how the features interact. Usually, without the bridge pattern, this will require us to refactor the code base.

In object-oriented programming, this is known as an exploding class hierarchy, but it can also happen in protocol-oriented programming as well.

Understanding the solution

The bridge pattern solves this problem by taking the interacting features and separating the functionality that is specific to each feature from the functionality that is shared between them. A bridge type can then be created, which will encapsulate the shared functionality, bringing them together.

Implementing the bridge pattern

To demonstrate how to use the bridge pattern, we will create two features. The first feature is a message feature that will store and prepare a message that will be sent out. The second feature is the sender feature that will send the message through a specific channel, such as email or SMS messaging.

Let's start off by creating two protocols named `Message` and `Sender`. The `Message` protocol will define the requirements for types that are used to create messages. The `Sender` protocol will be used to define the requirements for types that are used to send the messages through the specific channels. The following code shows how we would define these two protocols:

```
protocol Message {
    var messageString: String {get set}
    init(messageString: String)
    func prepareMessage()
}

protocol Sender {
    func sendMessage(message: Message)
}
```

The `Message` protocol defines one stored property named `messageString`, of the `String` type. This property will contain the text of the message and cannot be `nil`. One initiator and one method, named `prepareMessage()`, are also defined. The initiator will be used to set the `messageString` property and anything else required by the message type. The `prepareMessage()` method will be used to prepare the message prior to sending it. This method can be used to encrypt the message, add formatting, or do anything else to the message prior to sending it.

The `Sender` protocol defines one method named `sendMessage()`. This method will send the message through the channel defined by conforming types. In this function, we will need to ensure that the `prepareMessage()` method from the message type is called prior to sending the message.

Now, let's see how we can define two types that conform to the `Message` protocol:

```
class PlainTextMessage: Message {
    var messageString: String
    required init(messageString: String) {
        self.messageString = messageString
    }
    func prepareMessage() {
        //Nothing to do
    }
}

class DESEncryptedMessage: Message {
    var messageString: String
    required init(messageString: String) {
        self.messageString = messageString
    }
    func prepareMessage() {
        // Encrypt message here
        self.messageString = "DES: " + self.messageString
    }
}
```

Each of these types contains the required functionality to conform to the `Message` protocol. The only real difference between these types is in the `prepareMessage()` methods. In the `PlainTextMessage` class, the `prepareMessage()` method is empty because there is nothing to be done to the message prior to sending it. The `prepareMessage()` method of the `DESEncryptionMessage` class would normally contain the logic to encrypt the message, but, for this example, we will just prepend a *DES* tag to the beginning of the message, letting us know that this method was called.

Now let's create two types that will conform to the `Sender` protocol. These types would typically handle sending the message through a specific channel; however, in this example, we will simply print a message to the console:

```
class EmailSender: Sender{
    func sendMessage(message: Message) {
        print("Sending through E-Mail:")
        print(" \(message.messageString)")
    }
}
```

```
class SMSSender: Sender {
    func sendMessage(message: Message) {
        print("Sending through SMS:")
         print(" \(message.messageString)")
    }
}
```

Both the `EmailSender` and the `SMSSender` types conform to the `Sender` protocol by implementing the `sendMessage()` function.

These two features can now be used as shown in the following code:

```
var myMessage = PlainTextMessage(messageString: "Plain Text Message")
myMessage.prepareMessage()
var sender = SMSSender()
sender.sendMessage(message:myMessage)
```

This would work great, and code similar to this could be added anywhere it is needed to create and send a message. Now let's say that one day, a new requirement is received to add functionality that would verify the message prior to sending it to make sure it meets the requirements of the channel it is being sent through. To do this, we would start off by changing the `Sender` protocol to add the verify functionality, as follows:

```
protocol Sender {
    var message: Message? {get set}
    func sendMessage()
    func verifyMessage()
}
```

A new method named `verifyMessage()`, and a property named message were both added to the `Sender` protocol. The definition of the `sendMessage()` method was also changed. The original `Sender` protocol was designed to simply send the message. This new protocol is designed to verify the message prior to calling the `sendMessage()` function, and so we couldn't simply pass the message to the sender as we did in the previous definition.

The types that conform to the `Sender` protocol now need to change to conform to this new protocol. The following code shows how we would make these changes:

```
class EmailSender: Sender {
    var message: Message?
    func sendMessage() {
        print("Sending through E-Mail:")
        print("\(message!.messageString)")
    }
    func verifyMessage() {
```

```
            print("Verifying E-Mail message")
        }
}

class SMSSender: Sender {
    var message: Message?
    func sendMessage() {
        print("Sending through SMS:")
        print(" \(message!.messageString)")
    }
    func verifyMessage() {
        print("Verifying SMS message")
    }
}
```

The code that uses these types would now need to change since the types themselves have changed. The following example shows how these types would now be used:

```
var myMessage = PlainTextMessage(messageString: "Plain Text Message")
myMessage.prepareMessage()
var sender = SMSSender()
sender.message = myMessage
sender.verifyMessage()
sender.sendMessage()
```

These changes are not that hard to make; however, without the bridge pattern, we would need to refactor the entire code base and make the change everywhere that messages are being sent. The bridge pattern tells us that when we have two hierarchies that closely interact with each together, such as in this instance, we should put this interaction logic into a bridge type that will encapsulate the logic in one spot. This way, when we receive new requirements or enhancements, the change can be made in one spot, thereby limiting the refactoring that is required. We could make a bridge type for our message and sender hierarchies, as shown in the following example:

```
struct MessagingBridge {
    static func sendMessage(message: Message, sender: Sender) {
        var sender = sender
        message.prepareMessage()
        sender.message = message
        sender.verifyMessage()
        sender.sendMessage()
    }
}
```

Now, the logic of how the messaging and sender hierarchies interact is encapsulated into the `MessagingBridge` structure. Therefore, when the logic needs to change, the change can be made in this single type, meaning that we no longer have to refactor the entire code base.

The bridge pattern is a very good pattern to remember and use. There have been (and still are) times that I have regretted not using the bridge pattern in my code because, as we all know, requirements change frequently, and being able to make the changes in one spot rather than throughout the code base can save us a lot of time in the future.

Now, let's look at the next pattern in the structural category: the facade pattern.

The facade pattern

The facade pattern provides a simplified interface for a larger and more complex body of code. This allows us to make libraries easier to use and understand by hiding some of the complexities. It also allows us to combine multiple APIs into a single, easier-to-use API, which is what we will see in our example.

Understanding the problem

The facade pattern is often used when there is a complex system that has a large number of independent APIs that are designed to work together. Sometimes, it is hard to tell where the facade pattern should be used during the initial application design. The reason for this is that we normally try to simplify the initial API design. However, over time, and as requirements change and new features are added, the APIs become more and more complex. At this point, it becomes pretty evident where the facade pattern should have been used. A good rule to use is this: if you have several APIs that are working closely together to perform a task, you should consider using the facade pattern

Understanding the solution

The main idea of the facade pattern is to hide the complexity of the APIs behind a simple interface. This offers several advantages, the most obvious being that it simplifies how external code interacts with the APIs. It also promotes loose coupling, which allows the APIs to change without the need to refactor all the code that uses them.

Implementing the facade pattern

To demonstrate the facade pattern, we will create three APIs: `HotelBooking`, `FlightBooking`, and `RentalCarBooking`. These APIs will be used to search for and book hotels, flights, and rental cars for trips. While it would be very easy to call each of the APIs individually, we are going to create a `TravelFacade` structure that will consolidate the functionality of all three APIs into a single call.

Let's begin by defining the three APIs. We will start off by implementing the hotel API:

```
struct Hotel {
    //Information about hotel room
}

struct HotelBooking {
    static func getHotelNameForDates(to: NSDate, from: NSDate) ->
                                     [Hotel]? {
        let hotels = [Hotel]()
        //logic to get hotels
        return hotels
    }
    static func bookHotel(hotel: Hotel) {
        // logic to reserve hotel room
    }
}
```

The hotel API consists of `Hotel` and `HotelBooking` structures. The `Hotel` structure will be used to store the information about a hotel room. The `HotelBooking` structure will be used to search for and book the hotel rooms. The flight and rental car APIs are very similar to the hotel API. The following code shows both of them:

```
struct Flight {
    //Information about flights
}

struct FlightBooking {
    static func getFlightNameForDates(to: NSDate, from: NSDate) ->
                                      [Flight]? {
        let flights = [Flight]()
        //logic to get flights
        return flights
    }
    static func bookFlight(flight: Flight) {
        // logic to reserve flight
    }
}
struct RentalCar {
```

```
        //Information about rental cars
    }
    struct RentalCarBooking {
        static func getRentalCarNameForDates(to: NSDate, from: NSDate) ->
                                              [RentalCar]? {
            let cars = [RentalCar]()
            //logic to get cars
            return cars
        }
        static func bookRentalCar(rentalCar: RentalCar) {
            // logic to reserve rental car
        }
    }
```

In each of these APIs, there is a structure that is used to store information, and a structure that is used to provide the search/booking functionality. In the initial design, it would be very easy to call these individual APIs within our application. However, as we all know, requirements tend to change, which causes our APIs to change over time. By using the facade pattern here, we hide how the individual APIs are implemented.

Therefore, if we need to change how they work in the future, only the code in the facade type needs to change rather than the whole code base. This makes the code easier to maintain and update in the future. Now, let's look at how we will implement the facade pattern by creating a `TravelFacade` structure:

```
    struct TravelFacade {
        var hotels: [Hotel]?
        var flights: [Flight]?
        var cars: [RentalCar]?
        init(to: NSDate, from: NSDate) {
            hotels = HotelBooking.getHotelNameForDates(to: to, from: from)
            flights = FlightBooking.getFlightNameForDates(to: to, from: from)
            cars = RentalCarBooking.getRentalCarNameForDates(to: to,from: from)
        }
        func bookTrip(hotel: Hotel, flight: Flight, rentalCar: RentalCar) {
            HotelBooking.bookHotel(hotel: hotel)
            FlightBooking.bookFlight(flight: flight)
            RentalCarBooking.bookRentalCar(rentalCar: rentalCar)
        }
    }
```

The `TravelFacade` structure contains the functionality to search the three APIs and also book a hotel, flight, and rental car. This type can now be used to search for hotels, flights, and rental cars without having to directly access the individual APIs. This structure can also be used to book hotels, flights, and rental cars without having to access the individual APIs.

At the start of this chapter, we mentioned that it is not always obvious where the facade pattern should be used in the initial design. A good rule to follow is this: if we have several APIs that are working together to perform a task, the facade pattern should be considered.

Now, let's look at our last structural pattern, which is the proxy design pattern.

The proxy design pattern

With the proxy design pattern, one type will act as an interface for another type or API. This wrapper type, which is the proxy, can then add functionality to the object, hide the implementation of an API, or restrict access to the object.

Understanding the problem

The proxy pattern can be used to solve numerous problems, but I find that I mainly use this pattern to solve one of two problems.

The first problem that I use the proxy pattern for is when I want to create a layer of abstraction between a single API and my code. The API could be a local or remote API, but I usually use this pattern to put an abstraction layer between my code and a remote service. This will allow changes to the remote API without the need to refactor large portions of the code base.

The second problem that I use the proxy pattern to solve is when I need to make changes to an API but do not have the code, or there is already a dependency on the current API elsewhere in the application.

Understanding the solution

To solve these problems, the proxy pattern tells us that we should create a type that will act as an interface for interacting with the other API. In the example here, we will learn how to use the proxy pattern to add a layer of abstraction between our code and a remote API.

Implementing the proxy pattern

In this section, we will look at how we can use the proxy pattern to put a layer of abstraction between our code and a remote API. This will enable us to hide the implementation details of the remote API within the local proxy type. For this example, we will create a proxy type that will retrieve information from Apple's iTunes API.

For this example to work, we will need to implement the networking code within the proxy type to interact with Apple's iTunes API. While we will show the code, we will not cover how it works; instead, we are going to focus on how the proxy pattern is implemented.

To implement this pattern, we will begin by creating a type that will act as the proxy for the iTunes API. Since the networking part of the code will be asynchronous, we will use a closure to return the results when the iTunes API returns the results to the proxy type. The typealias for the closure is defined like this:

```
public typealias DataFromURLCompletionClosure = (Data?) -> Void
```

Next, let's create the proxy type, which we will name ITunesProxy:

```
public struct ITunesProxy {
    public func sendGetRequest (searchTerm: String, _ handler: @escaping
                                DataFromURLCompletionClosure) {
        let sessionConfiguration = URLSessionConfiguration.default
        var url = URLComponents()
        url.scheme = "https"
        url.host = "itunes.apple.com"
        url.path = "/search"
        url.queryItems = [
            URLQueryItem(name: "term", value: searchTerm),
        ]
        if let queryUrl = url.url {
            var request = URLRequest(url:queryUrl)
            request.httpMethod = "GET"
            let urlSession = URLSession(
                configuration:sessionConfiguration, delegate: nil,
                delegateQueue: nil)
            let sessionTask = urlSession.dataTask(with: request) {
                (data, response, error) in
                handler(data)
            }
            sessionTask.resume()
        }
    }
}
```

Once the proxy type is completed, it can be used anywhere in the code to access the iTunes API, like this:

```
let proxy = ITunesProxy()
proxy.sendGetRequest(searchTerm: "jimmy+buffett", {
    if let data = $0, let sString = String(data: data, encoding:
        String.Encoding(rawValue: String.Encoding.utf8.rawValue)) {
        print(sString)
    } else {
        print("Data is nil")
    }
})
```

This provides us with a layer of abstraction between the application code and the code needed to interact with the iTunes API. The biggest advantage that we get with the proxy pattern is that the implementation code to interact with the iTunes API is isolated in one type. This means, for example, that if Apple changes the URL from `https://www.apple.com/ itunes/` to `http://itunesapi.apple.com/`, or if anything else changes with the API calls, we will only need to make the change in one type.

Most experienced developers will recognize this pattern as one they have used in the past. It is common practice to create a layer of abstraction between code and remote APIs like this.

Now, let's look at behavioral design patterns.

Behavioral design patterns

Behavioral design patterns explain how types interact with each other. These patterns describe how different instances of types send messages to each other to make something happen.

There are nine well-known patterns that are part of the behavioral design pattern type. They are as follows:

- **Chain of responsibility:** This is used to process a variety of requests, each of which may be delegated to a different handler.
- **Command:** This creates objects that can encapsulate actions or parameters so that they can be invoked later or by a different component.
- **Iterator:** This allows us to access the elements of an object sequentially without exposing the underlying structure.

- **Mediator:** This is used to reduce coupling between types that communicate with each other.
- **Memento:** This is used to capture the current state of an object and store it in a manner that can be restored later.
- **Observer:** This allows an object to publish changes to its state. Other objects can then subscribe so that they can be notified of any
- **State:** This is used to alter the behavior of an object when its internal state changes.
- **Strategy:** This allows one out of a family of algorithms to be chosen at runtime.
- **Visitor:** This is a way of separating an algorithm from an object structure.

In this section, we are going to look at some examples of how to use strategy, observer, and command patterns in Swift. Let's start off by looking at the command pattern.

The command design pattern

The command design pattern lets us define actions that can be executed later. This pattern generally encapsulates all the information needed to call or trigger the actions later.

Understanding the problem

There are times when we need to separate the execution of a command from its invoker. Typically, this is when there is a type that needs to perform one of several actions; however, the choice of which action to use needs to be made at runtime

Understanding the solution

The command pattern tells us that we should encapsulate the logic for the various actions into a separate type that conforms to a command protocol. We can then provide instances of the command types for use by the invoker. The invoker will use the interface provided by the protocol to invoke the actions required.

Implementing the command pattern

In this section, we will demonstrate how to use the command pattern by implementing the logic for a simple calculator. To do this, we will start with a protocol that all the types that implement the math functions of the calculator must conform to. Let's name the protocol `MathCommand` and put the following code into it:

```
protocol MathCommand {
    func execute(num1: Double, num2: Double) -> Double
}
```

The `MathCommand` protocol requires one function to be implemented by any type that conforms to it. This function is named `execute()` and takes two parameters of the `Double` type and returns a value that is also of the Double type. The types that conform to this protocol will perform a mathematical function with the two parameters.

Now, we will create four types that conform to the `MathCommand` protocol. These types will be named `AdditionCommand`, `SubtractionCommand`, `MultiplicationCommand`, and `DivisionCommand`:

```
struct AdditionCommand: MathCommand {
    func execute(num1: Double, num2: Double) -> Double {
        return num1 + num2
    }
}

struct SubtractionCommand: MathCommand {
    func execute(num1: Double, num2: Double) -> Double {
        return num1 - num2
    }
}

struct MultiplicationCommand: MathCommand {
    func execute(num1: Double, num2: Double) -> Double {
        return num1 * num2
    }
}

struct DivisionCommand: MathCommand {
    func execute(num1: Double, num2: Double) -> Double {
        return num1 / num2
    }
}
```

Each of these command types conforms to the `MathCommand` protocol by implementing the `execute()` method. Within this method, we perform the mathematical function that the type's name implies.

We now need to create an invoker. This invoker will know how to execute any command that conforms to the `MathCommand` protocol. This will enable the calculator to perform any function that has a type that conforms to the `MathProtocol` associated with it. The following code shows how we would create such an invoker:

```
struct Calculator {
    func performCalculation(num1: Double, num2: Double,
                            command: MathCommand) -> Double{
        return command.execute(num1: num1, num2: num2)
    }
}
```

The `Calculator` type has one method named `performCalculation()`. This method accepts three parameters: two of the Double type and one of an instance of any type that conforms to the `MathCommand` protocol. Within the method, we return the results from the `execute()` method of the `MathCommand` instance using the two Double values passed into the method as parameters. Now, let's see how this works by using the calculator to solve the equation *(25 - 10) * 5*:

```
var calc = Calculator()
var startValue = calc.performCalculation(num1: 25, num2: 10, command:
SubtractionCommand())
var answer = calc.performCalculation(num1: startValue, num2: 5, command:
MultiplicationCommand())
```

We start off by creating an instance of the `Calculator` type. We then use the `performCalculation()` method to subtract 10 from 25, with the resulting value being 15. We do this by passing the values of 25 and 10 as the first two parameters of the `performCalculation()` method and then an instance of the `SubtractionCommand` type as the last parameter.

In the last line, we use the result from the first calculation, which was 15, and multiply it by 5. The final result will be 75.

There are several benefits to using the command pattern. One of the main benefits is that we are able to set which command to invoke at runtime, which also lets us swap the commands out with different implementations that conform to the command protocol as needed throughout the life of the application. Another advantage of the command pattern is that we encapsulate the details of the command implementations within the command types themselves rather than in the container type.

Now, let's look at the strategy pattern.

The strategy pattern

The strategy pattern is similar to the command pattern in that both are designed to decouple implementation details from the calling type. Both of these patterns also allow for the implementations to be swapped out at runtime. The big difference is that the strategy pattern is intended to encapsulate algorithms. When an algorithm is swapped out, the object is expected to perform the same functionality, but in a different way. In the command pattern, when the command was swapped out, it was expected to change the behavior of the object.

Understanding the problem

There are times in our applications when we need to change the backend algorithm that is used to perform an operation. Typically, this is when we have a type that has several different algorithms that can be used to perform the same task. However, the choice of which algorithm to use needs to be made at runtime.

Understanding the solution

The strategy pattern tells us that we should encapsulate the algorithm in a type that conforms to a strategy protocol. We can then provide instances of the strategy types for use by the invoker. The invoker will use the interface provided by the protocol to invoke the algorithm.

Implementing the strategy pattern

In this section, we will demonstrate the strategy pattern by showing how compression strategies can be swapped out at runtime. Let's begin this example by creating a `CompressionStrategy` protocol that each one of the compression types will conform to:

```
protocol CompressionStrategy {
    func compressFiles(filePaths: [String])
}
```

This protocol defines one method named `compressFiles()` that accepts a single parameter, which is an array of strings that contain the paths to the files that are to be compressed. Now, let's create two structures that conform to the `CompressionStrategy` protocol, named `ZipCompressionStrategy` and `RarCompressionStrategy`:

```
struct ZipCompressionStrategy: CompressionStrategy {
    func  compressFiles(filePaths: [String]) {
        print("Using Zip Compression")
    }
}

struct RarCompressionStrategy: CompressionStrategy {
    func compressFiles(filePaths: [String]) {
        print("Using RAR Compression")
    }
}
```

Both of these structures implement the `CompressionStrategy` protocol by implementing the method named `compressFiles()`, which accepts an array of strings. Within these methods, we simply print out the name of the compression that we are using. Normally, we would implement the compression logic in these methods.

Now, let's look at our `CompressContent` type, which will be called to compress the files:

```
struct CompressContent {
var strategy: CompressionStrategy
    func compressFiles(filePaths: [String]) {
        self.strategy.compressFiles(filePaths: filePaths)
    }
}
```

This type has one property named strategy that will contain an instance of a type that conforms to the `CompressStrategy` protocol. It also has one method named `compressFiles()` that accepts an array of strings that contain the paths to the files that we wish to compress. In this method, we compress the files by calling the `compressFiles(filePaths:)` method of the strategy instance.

We will use the `CompressContent` type as follows:

```
var filePaths = ["file1.txt", "file2.txt"]
var zip = ZipCompressionStrategy()
var rar = RarCompressionStrategy()

var compress = CompressContent(strategy: zip)
compress.compressFiles(filePaths: filePaths)

compress.strategy = rar
compress.compressFiles(filePaths: filePaths)
```

An array of strings is created that contains the files to compress. Instances of both the `ZipCompressionStrategy` and the `RarCompressionStrategy` strategy types are then created, as well as an instance of the `CompressContent` type. Initially, the compression strategy is set to the `ZipCompressionStrategy` instance and the `compressFiles()` method is called, which prints the Using `zip` compression message to the console. Then, the compression strategy is changed to the `RarCompressionStrategy` instance and the `compressFiles()` method is called again, which prints the Using `rar` compression message to the console.

The strategy pattern is good for setting the algorithms to use at runtime, which also lets us swap the algorithms out with different implementations as needed by the application. This pattern also allows us to encapsulate the details of the algorithm within the strategy types themselves, and not in the main implementation type.

Now, let's look at one last pattern, the observer pattern.

The observer pattern

The observer pattern is used to implement distributed event handling where an observer type is notified when an event occurs within another type. The observer pattern allows groups of objects to cooperate with one another with few dependencies between them. This pattern is so widely used that you have probably already come across it many times before if you have developed applications using any modern UI framework, such as Cocoa or Cocoa Touch.

Understanding the problem

There are times when we need to perform an action in one or more sections of our code when an event happens in another part of our code. This is a very common requirement with most modern UI frameworks, where we wish to be notified when the user has interacted with our user interface in some way.

Understanding the solution

With the observer pattern, the observer registers to be notified when an event happens. When the event is triggered, any instance that has registered for the event receives a notification that the event has occurred. There are several ways that we can implement the observer pattern in Swift, and, in this section, we will look at two of them. We are looking at multiple solutions for this pattern because each of these solutions helps us to implement the observer pattern under specific circumstances. We will talk about when to use each one of these solutions as we talk about the solutions themselves.

Implementing the observer pattern

For the first solution, we will use the `NotificationCenter` class. The `NotificationCenter` class provides us with a mechanism to register for, post, and receive notifications. All Cocoa-and Cocoa-Touch-based applications have a default notification center when they are running. There is no need to create our own instance of the `NotificationCenter` class.

When we use the notification center, we need to provide a name for each notification. One thing we never want to do is to hardcode the name in both the notifying type (the type that posts the notifications) and the receiving types (the types that receive the notifications).

Instead, we will want to define the name in a global constant and use it for both the notifying and the receiving types. Therefore, we will begin this example by defining the name for our notification as follows:

```
let NCNAME = "Notification Name"
```

Now, we will create the type that will post our notifications. In this example, our type will simply post a notification to the default notification center when we call a method named post:

```
class PostType {
    let nc = NotificationCenter.default
    func post() {
```

```
        nc.post(name: Notification.Name(rawValue: NCNAME), object: nil)
    }
}
```

Finally, we will create a type that will receive the notifications when they are posted to the notification center. This type will register a selector (in this example, a method named `receivedNotification()`) with the notification center that will be called when new notifications, identified by the name, are posted to the notification center:

```
class ObserverType {
    let nc = NotificationCenter.default
    init() {
        nc.addObserver(self,
            selector: #selector(receiveNotification(notification:)),
            name: Notification.Name(rawValue: NCNAME), object: nil)
    }
    @objc func receiveNotification(notification: Notification) {
        print("Notification Received")
    }
}
```

When we use `NotificationCenter`, we have to remember to prefix the method that will be called with the `@objc` attribute. The `@objc` attribute makes our Swift API available to the Objective-C runtime. This allows us to use the `receiveNotifications()` methods with `NotificationCenter`.

We can now use these types as follows:

```
var postType = PostType()
var observerType = ObserverType()
postType.post()
```

If we run this example, we will see that the **Notification Received** message from the `ObserverType` instance is printed to the console when we execute the `post()` method on the instance of the `PostType` type. Using the notification center is a very easy and quick way to add the observer pattern to your code.

If our notifier or observer types are written in Objective-C, then we should use the notification center as shown in this example. It is also easier to notify multiple recipients with the notification center than it is with the following solutions because that functionality is built into the notification center.

This second solution demonstrates how notifications are handled in the Cocoa and Cocoa Touch framework where we register an instance of a type, which conforms to a specific protocol, to receive notifications from instances of another type. In this example, we want to be notified when a zombie turns or spots us. Let's start by defining a protocol that any type that wants to receive the notifications must conform to. This protocol will be named `ZombieObserver`:

```
protocol ZombieObserver {
    func turnLeft()
    func turnRight()
    func seesUs()
}
```

This protocol will require that conforming types implement the three functions defined in the protocol. These will be the methods that are called to notify us when the zombie turns or spots us.

Now, let's define the observer that will receive the notifications from the `Zombie` type. We will name this class `MyObserver` and it will conform to the `ZombieObserver`, protocol so that it can receive the notifications when the zombie does something:

```
class MyObserver: ZombieObserver {
    func turnLeft() {
        print("Zombie turned left, we move right")
    }
    func turnRight() {
        print("Zombie turned right, we move left")
    }
    func seesUs() {
        print("Zombie sees us, RUN!!!!")
    }
}
```

Finally, we will implement the `Zombie` type. The `Zombie` type will send out notifications to the observer when it turns or spots someone:

```
struct Zombie {
    var observer: ZombieObserver
    func turnZombieLeft() {
        //Code to turn left
        //Notify observer
        observer.turnLeft()
    }
    func turnZombieRight() {
        //Code to turn right
        //Notify observer
```

```
        observer.turnRight()
    }
    func spotHuman() {
        //Code to lock onto a human
        //Notify observer
        observer.seesUs()
    }
}
```

In the `Zombie` type, we define one property that is of the `ZombieObserver` type. This is the instance that will receive the notifications when the zombie does something. Also in the `Zombie` type, we create three methods that are called when our zombie turns left, turns right, or spots a human. Note that in each of the methods, we notify the observer of the event that happened. Generally, these notifications would happen on new threads, but to simplify the code here, we took this code out.

We would use our `Zombie` and observer types as shown in the following example:

```
var observer = MyObserver()
var zombie = Zombie(observer: observer)

zombie.turnZombieLeft()
zombie.spotHuman()
```

When this code is run, `Zombie` turned left, we move right, and `Zombie` sees us. RUN!!!! messages from the `MyObserver` instance are printed to the console when the `turnZombieLeft()` and `spotHuman()` methods are called.

Implementing the observer pattern as shown in this example is the method used by most of the UI elements in the Cocoa and Cocoa Touch framework. If we need a single observer, this is usually the method we should use. If we need multiple observers, we could make our observer property an array of the `MyObserver` types, but then each time we notified the observers, we would need to loop through the array and notify each observer individually.

It is much easier to notify multiple observers using the `NSNotificationCenter` class because the logic to call multiple observers is already implemented for us.

Summary

Design patterns are solutions to software design problems that we tend to see over and over again in real-world application design. These patterns are designed to help us create reusable and flexible code. Design patterns can also make our code easier to read and understand for other developers and also for ourselves when we look back at our code months/years later.

If we look at the examples in this chapter carefully, we will notice that one of the backbones of design patterns is the protocol. Almost all design patterns (except the singleton design pattern) use protocols to help us create very flexible and reusable code.

If this was the first time that you have really looked at design patterns, you probably noticed some similarities to strategies that you have used in the past in your own code. This is expected when experienced developers are first introduced to design patterns. I would also encourage you to read more about design patterns because they will definitely help you to create more flexible and reusable code.

9
Case Studies

Ever since I bought my first computer, a Commodore Vic-20, I have been continuously learning new computer languages. I cannot count the number of computer languages that I have learned over the years. Even when I was working as a network engineer and security specialist, I learned languages such as Perl, Python, and shell scripting to automate administrative tasks. Learning all those languages has taught me that the best way to learn a new programming language or programming paradigm is to come up with several small projects and figure out how to implement them in the language or programming paradigm that you are trying to learn. With that in mind, for this chapter, we will look at two small projects and see how we can implement them using Swift and the protocol-oriented programming paradigm. I recommend that you read the requirements for the project and then try to implement your own solutions prior to reading the solution presented in this book. This will help you to think about application design using the protocol-oriented programming paradigm. I do have one tip for you: don't forget to use design patterns in your solutions.

In this chapter, you will learn the following topics:

- How to apply the protocol-oriented programming paradigm to real-world situations
- How to use design patterns with protocol-oriented programming to create real-world solutions

Protocol-oriented programming isn't just about using protocols, protocol extensions, and value types. If you are focused solely on using protocols and value types, then you are missing the main point of this programming paradigm. Protocol-oriented programming is about the overall design of the application or framework. Protocol-oriented programming with design patterns focuses on ensuring that we have a very flexible and easy-to-maintain code base that will enable us to very easily meet the needs of today and tomorrow.

Focusing on how we will maintain and expand our applications and frameworks in the future may seem like a waste of time with the tight deadlines we are always on; however, in the long-term, the time spent on making sure that our code base is easy to maintain and expand always ends up saving us time in the long run, as the requirements will change and new features will be added. We need to ensure that our code base is prepared for these changes.

In this chapter, we will be looking at two real-world case studies to see how we can apply the protocol-oriented paradigm with design patterns to write solutions for real-world projects. These two case studies are as follows:

- Creating a logging service for our applications
- Creating a data-access layer

In the first case study, we will look at how we can use the protocol-oriented programming paradigm to create a logging framework that can be easily maintained and expanded by our users. In the second case study, we will see how we can use the protocol-oriented programming paradigm to create a data access layer that is ready for different storage mediums.

Let's start by looking at how we can create a logging service for our application.

Logging services

If I kept a tally of the lines of code that I have written in each language over the course of my life, it would probably show that Java is the language that I have used the most. Java has its good and bad points, but one of the things that I really like about developing applications in Java is all the different logging frameworks that are available.

These logging frameworks make it incredibly effortless to turn on log messages, which makes debugging very easy while the application is being developed. These debugging messages can then be turned off when it is time to build the production release of the application. To do this, these logging frameworks let us define how and where we wish to log the messages for predefined log levels. Logging levels can also be ignored if we do not need them. The log levels range from Info (used purely for debugging), all the way up to Fatal (when something really bad happens).

Some of the logging frameworks that I have used with Java are **Log4j**, the **Java Logging API**, and **Apache Commons Logging**. For this project, we will create a logging service similar to these, but with the Swift language. The first thing we need to do is to define the requirements for our logging service.

Requirements

Our logging service has several requirements, as defined in the following list:

- We will need to have multiple log levels. The log levels that our framework will support are **Fatal**, **Error**, **Warn**, **Debug**, and **Info**.
- We will need to have multiple logging profiles. The framework will define two profiles by default: `LoggerNull` and `LoggerConsole`. The `LoggerNull` profile will do nothing with the log message (it will pretty much ignore the message and not log it anywhere), while the `LoggerConsole` profile will print the log message to the console.
- The user will have the ability to add their own logging profile so that they can log messages to a database, a `UILabel`, or any other location they want.
- We must have the ability to configure the logging framework when the application starts, and keep that configuration throughout the life cycle of the application. We do not want to force the users of our framework to reconfigure the framework every time they need to use it.
- We can assign multiple logger profiles to a single log level to give the user the ability to display or store the logs to multiple profiles.

Before reading further, based on these requirements, note the type of design that you come up with. Once you have worked out your design, then continue reading and compare your design with the one presented here.

The design

We are going to separate the design into two sections. The first section will be the *logger profile* section that will contain the types that will do the actual logging of the messages to a storage medium or display them. The second section will be the *logger* section that will contain the types that the applications interface with. The logger types will determine the log level of the message and then pass the message to the appropriate logger profiles to log the message. Let's start off by looking at the logger profile section.

We will begin the logger profile design by creating a protocol named `LoggerProfile`. This protocol will define the interface that the logger profiles will present, and any type that conforms to this protocol can be used to log messages. The out-of-the-box framework will provide two types that will conform to the `LoggerProfile` protocol. These types will be of the `LoggerNull` and `LoggerConsole` types.

By starting the design with the `LoggerProfile` protocol and using the interface exposed by the protocol to write log messages to the display/storage medium, we are employing the concept of polymorphism. This will allow the users of our framework to add additional logging profiles by creating types that conform to the `LoggerProfile` protocol. These types provide a means to log messages to any display or storage medium that meets their requirements, such as a database, file, or even `UILabel`.

Let's look at a diagram that shows how we implement this design. The diagram shows that we extend the `LoggerProfile` protocol to add a method named `getCurrentDateString()`. This method will return a formatted string that contains the current date and time. The diagram also shows that the `LoggerNull` and `LoggerConsole` types will conform to the `LoggerProfile` protocol:

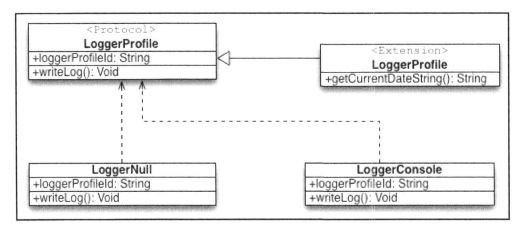

Let's look at how we implement this design. We will start off by looking at the `LoggerProfile` protocol and the `LoggerProfile` protocol extension:

```
protocol LoggerProfile {
    var loggerProfileId: String {get}
    func writeLog(level: String, message: String)
}

extension LoggerProfile {
```

```
func getCurrentDateString() -> String{
    let date = Date()
    let dateFormatter = DateFormatter()
    dateFormatter.dateFormat = "MM/dd/yyyy hh:mm"
    return dateFormatter.string(from: date)
}
}
```

The `LoggerProfile` protocol defines one property and one function. The property is named `loggerProfileId`, which is of the `String` type. This property is used to uniquely identify the logging profile. This property will be used in the framework to ensure that the logger profile is not added to the log level more than once. The method defined in the protocol is named `writeLog()` and will be called to write the log message to the display or storage medium defined by the profile.

We created a protocol extension for the `LoggerProfile` protocol, which adds a method named `getCurrentDateString()`. This method returns a formatted date string of the current date and time. While types that conform to the `LoggerProfile` protocol can elect not to use the `getCurrentDateString()` method provided by the protocol extension, it is recommended that they do use this method in order to ensure that all the logger profile types provide a date and time string with a consistent format.

Now, let's look at the `LoggerNull` and `LoggerConsole` types:

```
struct LoggerNull: LoggerProfile {
    let loggerProfileId = "hoffman.jon.logger.null"
    func writeLog(level: String, message: String) {
        // Do nothing
    }
}

struct LoggerConsole: LoggerProfile {
    let loggerProfileId = "hoffman.jon.logger.console"
    func writeLog(level: String, message: String) {
        let now = getCurrentDateString()
        print("\(now): \(level) - \(message)")
    }
}
```

Both logger profiles have a unique ID defined in the `loggerProfileId` constant. Reverse DNS name notation is used as the format for this ID. Reverse DNS notation is a naming convention that is commonly used for naming components, packages, and other types. A reverse DNS notation string is usually based on a registered domain name, but the names are in reverse order. For these examples, I am using my name rather than a registered domain name.

We also provide, for both types, an implementation of the `writeLog()` method that is required by the `LoggerProfile` protocol. For the `LoggerNull` type, the `writeLog()` method does not do anything with the message because this type is written so that it ignores any messages, as if the messages were being sent to `/dev/null`. The `writeLog()` method for the `LoggerConsole` type retrieves a string that represents the current date and time using the `getCurrentDateString()` method provided by the `LoggerProfile` protocol extension, and then writes the log message to the console.

The next part of our logger service will be of the `Logger` type. This type will keep track of which logger profiles are assigned to the various log levels. Applications will primarily use the interface provided by the `Logger` protocol as the means to configure the logger service and to log messages.

While the initial design of the framework only contains one type that conforms to the `Logger` protocol, we will still begin this design with a protocol to give us the ability to add additional types that conform to the `logger` profile in the future. It will also allow the users to add additional types that conform to the `logger` profile if they want. It may not seem like that big of a deal right now, but two or three years down the road, as requirements change and new features are added, we will be glad that a protocol was used here.

Let's begin by defining the log levels that our framework will offer. We will use an enumeration to define these levels, as there is a finite number of these levels. The following enumeration defines the log levels for our logging framework:

```
enum LogLevels: String {
    case fatal
    case error
    case warn
    case debug
    case info
    static let allValues = [fatal, error, warn, debug, info]
}
```

The `LogLevels` enumeration defines five log levels. It also provides an array that contains all five levels. This array can be used to retrieve all the log levels if needed. Now, let's look at the `Logger` protocol:

```
protocol Logger {
    static var loggers: [LogLevels:[LoggerProfile]] {get set}
    static func writeLog(logLevel: LogLevels, message: String)
}
```

The `Logger` protocol defines one property, named `loggers`, of the `Dictionary` type. This `Dictionary` has a log level that is defined in the `LogLevels` enumeration as the key and an array of types that conform to the `LoggerProfile` protocol as the value. We also define one method in the `Logger` protocol named `writeLog()`. This method is called within the application to write a message to the logs. This method takes two arguments: the first argument is the log level to write the log message, and the second is the log message itself.

We define both the `loggers` property and the `writeLog()` method as static so that they can be accessed without having to create an instance of the `Logger` type. Properties and methods that are defined with the static keyword are known as type properties and type methods. Another reason these are created as static is because one of the requirements for the logger framework is to be able to configure the framework once, and have the ability to keep that configuration throughout the life cycle of the application. By creating these as static, there will be one and only one instance of them throughout the life cycle of the application, thereby fulfilling this requirement. We could use the singleton pattern to fulfill this requirement; however, using type methods/properties would seem to work better in this situation. We will see the advantage of this when we look at how we will use our logging framework.

Now, let's look at the methods that the `Logger` protocol extension provides to types that conform to the `Logger` protocol. The protocol extension will provide six type (static) methods:

- `logLevelContainsProfile(logLevel: LogLevels, loggerProfile: LoggerProfile) ->Bool`: This will check the log level and return true if it already contains the logger profile
- `setLogLevel(logLevel: LogLevels, loggerProfile: LoggerProfile)`: This adds a logger profile to the log level
- `addLogProfileToAllLevels(defaultLoggerProfile: LoggerProfile)`: This will add the logger profile to all log levels
- `removeLogProfileFromLevel(logLevel: LogLevels, loggerProfile: LoggerProfile)`: This removes the logger profile from the log level if it is defined for that level
- `removeLogProfileFromAllLevels(loggerProfile: LoggerProfile)`: This removes the log profile from all log levels
- `hasLoggerForLevel(logLevel: LogLevels) ->Bool`: This returns `true` if there is any logger profile configured for the log level; otherwise, it returns `false`

Let's look at the code for the individual methods, starting with the
`logLevelContainsProfile()` method:

```
static func logLevelContainsProfile(logLevel: LogLevels, loggerProfile:
LoggerProfile) -> Bool {
    if let logProfiles = loggers[logLevel] {
        for logProfile in logProfiles where
            logProfile.loggerProfileId == loggerProfile.loggerProfileId {
                return true
        }
    }
    return false
}
```

This method will return `true` if the log level contains the logger profile, and will be used by
the `setLogLevel()` and `addLogProfileToAllLevels()` methods to ensure that we do
not add a logger profile to a log level more than once. This method starts off by using
optional binding to retrieve a list of logger profiles assigned to the log level. The for-in
statement is used with a where clause to loop through the list of logger profiles where the
`loggerProfileId` property matches the `loggerProfileId` property of the profile it is
looking for. If any item in the array matches this property, the method returns `true`;
otherwise it returns `false`.

Next, let's look at the `setLogLevel()` method:

```
static func setLogLevel(logLevel: LogLevels, loggerProfile: LoggerProfile)
{
    if let _ = loggers[logLevel] {
        if !logLevelContainsProfile(logLevel: logLevel,
                                    loggerProfile: loggerProfile) {
            loggers[logLevel]?.append(loggerProfile)
        }
    } else {
        var a = [LoggerProfile]()
        a.append(loggerProfile)
        loggers[logLevel] = a
    }
}
```

The `setLogLevel()` method uses the `logLevelContainsProfile()` method to verify that the logger profile is not already assigned to the specified log level; if it isn't, then it will add the logger profile to that level. This method begins by using optional binding to retrieve the list of logger profiles assigned to the log level. This is done to verify that there is a valid array assigned to the log level. The `logLevelContainsProfile()` method is used to verify that the logger profile is not already assigned to the level and, if it is not, then it is added.

If the optional binding fails at the start of the method, then a new array is created, the logger profile is added to this new array, and the array is assigned to the log level within the loggers dictionary.

Next, let's look at the `addLogProfileToAllLevels()` method:

```
static func addLogProfileToAllLevels( defaultLoggerProfile: LoggerProfile)
{
    for level in LogLevels.allValues {
        setLogLevel(logLevel: level, loggerProfile:
        defaultLoggerProfile)
    }
}
```

The `addLogProfileToAllLevels()` method is used to add a logger profile to all the log levels. This can be used to initialize the logger framework by adding a single profile to all the levels. This method loops through each of the log levels and then calls the `setLogLevel()` method to try to add the logger profile to each individual log level.

The next method we will look at is the `removeLogProfileFromLevel()` method:

```
static func removeLogProfileFromLevel(logLevel: LogLevels, loggerProfile:
LoggerProfile) {
    if var logProfiles = loggers[logLevel] {
        if let index = logProfiles.firstIndex(where:
                {$0.loggerProfileId == loggerProfile.loggerProfileId}) {
            logProfiles.remove(at: index)
        }
        loggers[logLevel] = logProfiles
    }
}
```

The `removeLogProfileFromLevel()` method will remove the logger profile from the specified log level. This method starts off by using optional binding to retrieve the list of logger profiles for the log level. The `indexOf()` method is used to locate the index of the logger profile that matches the logger profile that needs to be removed. If the profile is found, it is removed.

The next method is the removeLogProfileFromAllLevels() method:

```
static func removeLogProfileFromAllLevels(loggerProfile: LoggerProfile) {
    for level in LogLevels.allValues {
        removeLogProfileFromLevel(logLevel: level, loggerProfile:
        loggerProfile)
    }
}
```

The removeLogProfileFromAllLevels() method will attempt to remove a logger profile from all the log levels. This method will loop through all of the log levels that have been defined and call the removeLogProfileFromLevel() method in an attempt to remove the logger profile from that level.

The final method in the Logger protocol extension is the hasLoggerForLevel() method:

```
static func hasLoggerForLevel(logLevel: LogLevels) -> Bool {
    guard let _ = loggers[logLevel] else {
        return false
    }
    return true
}
```

The hasLoggerForLevel() method returns true if the log level contains any logger profiles; otherwise, it returns false. This method uses optional binding with a guard statement to retrieve the list of logger profiles assigned to the log level. If the optional binding statement fails, then a false value is returned; otherwise, a true value is returned.

Now, let's look at our Logger type, which will conform to the Logger protocol:

```
struct MyLogger: Logger {
    static var loggers = [LogLevels: [LoggerProfile]]()
    static func writeLog(logLevel: LogLevels, message: String) {
        guard hasLoggerForLevel(logLevel: logLevel) else {
            print("No logger")
            return
        }
        if let logProfiles = loggers[logLevel] {
            for logProfile in logProfiles {
                logProfile.writeLog(level: logLevel.rawValue,
                                    message: message)
            }
        }
    }
}
```

The `MyLogger` type has one property named `loggers`, which is a dictionary whose key is a log level defined in the `LogLevels` enumeration and whose value is an array of types that conform to the `LoggerProfile` protocol. The `writeLog()` method is used within the applications to write a message to the log, and it takes two arguments. The arguments are the log level to write the log message for and the log message itself.

The `MyLogger` type can be used as follows:

```
MyLogger.addLogProfileToAllLevels(defaultLoggerProfile: LoggerConsole())
MyLogger.writeLog(logLevel: LogLevels.debug, message: "Debug Message 1")
MyLogger.writeLog(logLevel:  LogLevels.error,  message:  "Error  Message
1")
```

This sample code begins by adding the `LoggerConsole` logger profile to all the log levels. This will cause all the log messages, no matter what the log level is, to be logged to the console. The `Debug` log level is then used to log the `Debug Message 1` message, which will be written to the console. Finally, the `Error` log level is used to log the `ErrorMessage 1` message. This message will also be written to the console.

If you are familiar with the design patterns from `Chapter 8`, *Adopting Design Patterns with Swift*, you will recognize that we are using the command pattern with this solution. The command pattern lets us define actions that can be executed later by encapsulating the logic of the action into a type. In this solution, we'll define the logic to execute into the logger profile types. Then, the `Logger` type will execute the logic when needed.

In this example, we can see that we do not need to create an instance of the `Logger` type to configure it or to log messages. The reason for this is that we made the properties and methods static (type methods and type properties). When we are creating frameworks that should have a very small footprint—then for instance, this logger framework—using type methods and properties to avoid instantiation of the types can make the frameworks significantly easier to use.

Conclusion

The basis of both the logger profiles and the loggers themselves are protocols, therefore making it easy to add additional profiles and loggers by creating new types that conform to these protocols. Protocol extensions are used to add functionality to types that conform to the protocol. These new types also automatically receive the functionality defined within the protocol extensions. Designing frameworks in this manner allows us to very easily add functionality and new features as we receive new requirements. It also allows the users of the framework to expand it to suit their needs.

When designing frameworks or applications, one thing that all good architects keep in the backs of their mind is not only how to implement the current requirements, but also how they can expand the framework or application to meet future needs. This is the idea behind using protocols and using the interface provided by the protocol, rather than concrete types. Using the interface provided by the protocol gives you the ability to use any type that conforms to the protocol. This adds a lot of flexibility and expandability to our frameworks and applications.

Now, let's look at how we can create a data access layer that can be easily expanded to use different data storage mediums.

The data access layer

The most serious applications need to persist certain amounts of data. This data could be transactional data, user preferences, or the current state of the application. There are many ways in which data can be persisted in our applications. Determining the appropriate way to persist this data can be one of the most critical decisions that an architect needs to make.

As an architect, we should separate the actual data storage from the business logic. This will allow the application to change how the data is persisted in the future without having to change the business logic. This separation creates what is called a **data access layer**.

When designing an application, it is important to design a good data access layer because having a good data access layer will make the code much easier to maintain as the requirements change. If we separate the data-access layer from the main business logic, then if the backend data store changes, only the code within the data-access layer needs to change.

Requirements

Our data-access layer will have several requirements:

- All access to the backend data storage should go through the data helper types. These data helper types will handle all the **create**, **read**, **update**, **and delete** (**CRUD**) functionalities to the backend storage.
- Code external to this data-access layer should not know how the data is persisted.

- For our example, we will need to create two types—one named player, which will contain information about a baseball player, and one named team, which will contain information about a baseball team. Each baseball player will contain the team ID and information about the team that they play for.
- For our example, we will store the data in an array; however, we will need the ability to change the storage mechanism without having to touch our business logic code.

Before reading further, based on these requirements, try to figure out what type of design you need for this. Once you have worked out your design, continue reading and compare your design to the one we present.

The design

The data-access layer will consist of three layers. The bottom-most layer, known as the **data helper layer**, will consist of types that will be used to persist the data. For this example, the data will be stored in an array, but these types should be easily updatable to persist the data in any way we need in the future.

The next layer is the **data model layer**, which will contain tuples that model how the data is stored in the data helper layer pretty closely. These tuples will be used as temporary storage to read and write data to/from the data store. Some people prefer using structures at the model layer, but I find that tuples work just as well because these types should not contain any business logic.

The final layer is the **bridge layer**, which converts the data from the business logic layer into the data-access layer. The bridge layer is the layer that separates our business logic from the data access logic. This layer will contain types that our business logic will use to access the data, and will contain bridge types that will convert the data types used in the business access layer to the data types used in the data-access layer.

In this example, there will be two types of data stored in two tables. These will be the Teams and the Players tables. From the preceding description, this means that two data helper classes are needed (`TeamDataHelper` and `PlayerDataHelper`) with two tuples (`Team` and `Player`).

The data-access layer design will look like this:

Bridge Layer	PlayerBridge / Player	TeamBridge / Team
Data Model Layer	PlayerData	TeamData
Data Helper Layer	PlayerDataHelper	TeamDataHelper

Let's start off by looking at the data model layer, since it will be the communication layer between the bridge layer and the data helper layer.

The data model layer

There are two types defined in the data model layer. These types are used to transfer the data between the data helper layer and the bridge layer. Since these types should be used exclusively to transfer the data, using value types and, in particular, tuples is preferred. Keep in mind that we want to avoid tightly coupling the business logic with the data-access layer; therefore, these types should not be used outside the data-access layer. If we avoid tightly coupling the business logic with the data-access layer, we will have the ability to change either one independently of the other. The following code shows the types in the data model layer:

```
typealias TeamData = ( teamId: Int64?, city: String?, nickName: String?,
                       abbreviation: String?)
typealias PlayerData = ( playerId: Int64?, firstName: String?,
                         lastName: String?, number: Int?,
                         teamId: Int64?, position: Positions?)
```

We will have a bridge that will convert the data from these types into data structures used by the business logic layer. We will implement these bridges later in this section.

In the `Player` tuple, there is an element named position of the `Positions` type. The `Positions` type is an enumeration that contains all the valid positions that a player can play. The following code shows how to define the `Positions` type:

```
enum Positions: String {
    case pitcher = "Pitcher"
    case catcher = "Catcher"
    case firstBase = "First Base"
```

```
        case secondBase = "Second Base"
        case thirdBase = "Third Base"
        case shortstop = "Shortstop"
        case leftField = "Left Field"
        case centerField = "Center Field"
        case rightField = "Right field"
        case designatedHitter = "Designated Hitter"
    }
```

Now let's look at our data helper layer that will be used to persist our data.

The data helper layer

In a design such as this, we need to have good error checking, which will let external code know when something bad happens; therefore, we will start the data helper layer by defining the errors that can be thrown. Swift's error-handling framework will be used which means that the errors are defined in an enumeration, as follows:

```
enum DataAccessError: Error {
    case datastoreConnectionError
    case insertError
    case deleteError
    case searchError
    case nilInData
}
```

We will see how these errors are thrown as we go through the code. Depending on the type of persistence that is used, the error types may change to give more details about the actual errors that occurred.

The data helper layer will be used to persist the data. This is the layer that will change as our storage mechanism changes. In this example, the data will be stored in an array; however, the types in this layer should have the ability to change as different storage mechanisms are needed in the future. This layer will contain one type for each data type in our data model layer. These types will be used to read and write the data.

We will begin by creating a `DataHelper` protocol that will define the minimum set of methods that each data helper type must implement.

The `DataHelper` protocol looks as follows:

```
protocol DataHelper {
    associatedtype T
    static func insert(_ item: T) throws -> Int64
    static func delete(_ item: T) throws -> Void
    static func findAll() throws -> [T]?
}
```

Within this protocol, we define three methods. These are as follows:

- `insert`: This inserts a row into the table
- `delete`: This deletes a row from the table
- `findAll`: This returns all the rows in the table

There is only one method that is defined to query the data. This is done because the methods to query each individual data type may vary depending on the data; therefore, the method(s) needed to query these types could be different. We need to evaluate the query method(s) needed for each data type on an individual basis.

Now let's build the `TeamDataHelper` type that will conform to the `DataHelper` protocol. This type will be used to persist the team data:

```
struct  TeamDataHelper:  DataHelper  {
    //  Code  goes  here
}
```

This type starts by defining an `associatedtype` and then creates an array to store the data in the following:

```
typealias T = TeamData
static var teamData: [T] = []
```

The `teamData` array is defined as static, so there will be one and only one instance of this array in the code. The `typealias T` variable is set to the `TeamData` type. Now, let's look at how we can implement each of the three methods defined in the `DataHelper` protocol, plus one extra method that will search the data by its unique identifier of the team. We will not discuss the implementation details here, because we are more concerned with the design than how we store/search the information in an array.

The first method that we will implement is the `insert()` method, which will insert an item into the array. This method will return an `Int64` value representing the unique ID of the item if everything was stored properly. This method will also throw an error if there is an issue with the data. If another storage mechanism was being used, then this method may need to throw additional errors:

```
static func insert(_ item: T) throws -> Int64 {
    guard item.teamId != nil && item.city != nil && item.nickName !=
        nil && item.abbreviation != nil else {
            throw DataAccessError.nilInData
    }
    teamData.append(item)
    return item.teamId!
}
```

Now, let's create the `delete()` function to remove an item from the array. This method will throw an error if the item does not exist or if the `teamId` is `nil`:

```
static func delete (_ item: T) throws -> Void {
    guard let id = item.teamId else {
        throw DataAccessError.nilInData
    }
    let teamArray = teamData
    for (index, team) in teamArray.enumerated() where team.teamId == id {
        teamData.remove(at: index)
        return
    }
    throw DataAccessError.deleteError
}
```

Now, let's implement the `findAll()` method, which will return all of the teams in the array. This method can throw an error, but that is more for future needs:

```
static func findAll() throws -> [T]? {
    return teamData
}
```

Finally, the `find()` method is implemented to search and return a single item from the team array. We may need additional `find()` methods depending on our needs, but this method will return the team with the particular `teamId`. This method is also marked to throw an error, but it is also for future needs. If the `teamId` is not found in the array, it will return a `nil` value:

```
static func find(_ id: Int64) throws -> T? {
    for team in teamData where team.teamId == id {
        return team
```

```
    }
    return nil
}
```

The `PlayerDataHelper` type is implemented just like the `TeamDataHelper` type. To see the code for the `PlayerDataHelper` class, please download the code from the Packt website.

Ideally, for the data access layer, the data (`PlayerData` and `TeamData`) and data helper (`PlayerDataHelper` and `TeamDataHelper`) types would be decoupled from the main business logic. If we look through the design patterns that we discussed earlier in this book, we can see that the bridge pattern can be used here. Let's see how we can use the bridge pattern to maintain a good separation layer between our data-access layer, and our application code.

We will want to start off by defining how to model the data within the application itself. This data can be modeled exactly like the data model within the data-access layer or it can be designed significantly differently.

 I usually find that if I properly normalize my data, then there will be significant differences between how I store the data and how I use it within my application. By separating our data-access layer from our application code, we will also able to model our data differently between these two layers.

Let's now look at how we will design our bridge layer.

The bridge layer

In this example, the data in the data-access layer and the application layer will have only one small difference: when a player is retrieved, the information about the team will be retrieved with it and will be a part of the player's data structure. Let's see how we can define the team and the player in the bridge layer. Let's start off by defining the `Team` type, because it is needed within the `Player` type:

```
struct  Team  {
    var  teamId:   Int64?
    var  city:  String?
    var  nickName:String?
    var  abbreviation:String?
}
```

Value types are being used for the data structures in this example. When we use value types for data structures in this way, we need to remember that changes to these types are only persisted in the scope that the changes are made in. If we need to persist the changes outside the scope that the changes were made in, we must use inout parameters. Ultimately, the choice between using a value or reference type is yours; the key is to be consistent and document the type used.

In this example, the Team structure is designed to mirror the TeamData tuple that represents the teams in the data helper layer. Now let's look at the Player structure:

```
struct Player {
    var playerId: Int64?
    var firstName: String?
    var lastName: String?
    var number: Int?
    var teamId: Int64? {
        didSet {
            if let t = try? TeamBridge.retrieve(teamId!) {
                team = t
            }
        }
    }
    var position: Positions?
    var team: Team?
    init(playerId: Int64?, firstName: String?, lastName: String?, number:
    Int?, teamId: Int64?, position: Positions?) {
        self.playerId = playerId
        self.firstName = firstName
        self.lastName = lastName
        self.number = number
        self.teamId = teamId
        self.position = position
        if let id = self.teamId {
            if let t = try? TeamBridge.retrieve(id) {
                team = t
            }
        }
    }
}
```

The `Player` structure is similar to the `PlayerData` tuple, except that an additional optional property of the `Team` type is added. This property will hold the information about the team that the player is on. We use a property observer to load the information about the team from the data store whenever the `teamId` property is set. We also load the team information in the initializer. Remember that the property observers are not called during the initialization of a type; therefore, the `didSet` observer is not called when we set `teamId` during initialization.

Now, let's look at the bridge types that will be used as a bridge between our data-access layer and our application code. We will start off by looking at our `TeamBridge` structure:

```
struct TeamBridge {
    static func save(_ team: inout Team) throws {
        let teamData = toTeamData(team)
        let id = try TeamDataHelper.insert(teamData)
        team.teamId = id
    }
    static func delete(_ team: Team) throws {
        let teamData = toTeamData(team)
        try TeamDataHelper.delete(teamData)
    }
    static func retrieve(_ id: Int64) throws -> Team? {
        if let t = try TeamDataHelper.find(id) {
            return toTeam(t)
        }
        return nil
    }
    static func toTeamData(_ team: Team) -> TeamData {
        return TeamData(teamId: team.teamId , city: team.city, nickName:
        team.nickName, abbreviation: team.abbreviation)
    }
    static func toTeam(_ teamData: TeamData) -> Team {
        return Team(teamId: teamData.teamId, city: teamData.city, nickName:
        teamData.nickName, abbreviation: teamData.abbreviation)
    }
}
```

The `TeamBridge` structure has five methods. The first three methods use the functionality from the `TeamDataHelper` structure to insert, delete, and retrieve data from the data-access layer. Note that in the `save()` method, an `inout` parameter is used because we are making changes to the team parameter that we want to persist outside of the scope for this method. The last two methods will convert the data between the `TeamData` tuple (data-access layer) and the `Team` class (application layer).

Now, if (or when) requirements change, we can change either the data-access layer or the application layer independently of each other. The bridge structure may need to change as either the data-access layer or the application layer changes, but it is a lot easier to make this single bridge type rather than refactoring the entire code base.

Now let's look at the `PlayerBridge` structure:

```
struct PlayerBridge {
    static func save(_ player: inout Player) throws {
        let playerData = toPlayerData(player)
        let id = try PlayerDataHelper.insert(playerData)
        player.playerId = id
    }
    static func delete(_ player:Player) throws {
        let playerData = toPlayerData(player)
        try PlayerDataHelper.delete(playerData)
    }
    static func retrieve(_ id: Int64) throws -> Player? {
        if let p = try PlayerDataHelper.find(id) {
            return toPlayer(p)
        }
        return nil
    }
    static func toPlayerData(_ player: Player) -> PlayerData {
        return PlayerData(playerId: player.playerId, firstName:
        player.firstName, lastName: player.lastName, number: player.number,
        teamId: player.teamId, position: player.position)
    }
    static func toPlayer(_ playerData: PlayerData) -> Player {
        return Player(playerId: playerData.playerId, firstName:
        playerData.firstName, lastName: playerData.lastName, number:
        playerData.number, teamId: playerData.teamId, position:
        playerData.position)
    }
}
```

The `PlayerBridge` structure is very similar to the `TeamBridge` structure, except that we are converting between the `PlayerData` tuple (data-access layer) and the `Player` class (application layer). Once again, this allows us to change either the data-access layer or the application layer independently of each other.

Using the data-access layer

Now let's see how to use the data-access layer by creating a team and a player:

```
var bos = Team( teamId: 0, city: "Boston",
                nickName: "Red Sox", abbreviation: "BOS")

try? TeamBridge.save(&bos)
var ortiz = Player( playerId: 0, firstName: "David",
                lastName: "Ortiz", number: 34, teamId: bos.teamId,
                position: Positions.designatedHitter)

try? PlayerBridge.save(&ortiz)
```

In this code, we created one team, the `BostonRedSox`, and one player, `DavidOrtiz`. We also put `DavidOrtiz` on the `BostonRedSox` team by assigning `RedSoxteamid` to the player's team id. This information can now be retrieved, as shown in the following code:

```
if let team = try? TeamBridge.retrieve(0) {
    print("--- \(team.city)")
}

if let player = try? PlayerBridge.retrieve(0) {
    print("---- \(player.firstName) \(player.lastName) plays for
        \(player.team?.city)")
}
```

This code will print out the following results:

```
--- Optional("Boston")")
---- Optional("David")") Optional("Ortiz")") plays for Optional("Boston")")
```

By using the `TeamBridge` and `PlayerBridge` types, we do not need to be concerned about how the data is being stored in the backend; it can use an SQLite database, an array, or even a file to store the information. We are also able to change the backend storage independently of the main application code. This will allow us to change the backend storage to meet any new requirements that we may have in the future, without having to refactor all the main application code.

Conclusion

Creating separate layers, as we showed in this example, may take additional time when we initially build our application, but it will save us time in the long term because requirements will change and new features will be added; therefore, our code needs to be easy to change in order to meet these needs. Creating separate layers, and using the bridge pattern to connect these layers, gives us the ability to change each of the layers easily and independently of the others.

Summary

In this chapter, we looked at two case studies to see how we can use Swift with the protocol-oriented programming paradigm and how we can use design patterns to create easy-to-maintain and flexible applications. If you worked through the designs yourself and your design was different from the ones presented here, that is OK; there are many correct answers for each of these problems. The key is to make sure your applications are designed so that they are easily maintained and very flexible.

As an architect, your focus should not only be on meeting the requirements of your framework or application, but also on making your code base easy to maintain and expand in order to meet future requirements. Using a programming paradigm such as protocol-oriented programming, and emphasizing the use of design patterns in our application's design, can help us meet these requirements.

Other Books You May Enjoy

If you enjoyed this book, you may be interested in these other books by Packt:

Mastering Swift 5 – Fifth Edition

Jon Hoffman

ISBN: 9781789139860

- Understand core Swift components, including operators, collections, control flows, and functions
- Learn how and when to use classes, structures, and enumerations
- Understand how to use protocol-oriented design with extensions to write easier-to-manage code
- Use design patterns with Swift, to solve commonly occurring design problems
- Implement copy-on-write for you custom value types to improve performance
- Add concurrency to your applications using Grand Central Dispatch and Operation Queues
- Implement generics to write flexible and reusable code

Hands-On Design Patterns with Swift

Giordano Scalzo, Florent Vilmart, Sergio De Simone

ISBN: 9781789135565

- Work efficiently with Foundation and Swift Standard library
- Understand the most critical GoF patterns and use them efficiently
- Use Swift 4.2 and its unique capabilities (and limitations) to implement and improve GoF patterns
- Improve your application architecture and optimize for maintainability and performance
- Write efficient and clean concurrent programs using futures and promises, or reactive programming techniques
- Use Swift Package Manager to refactor your program into reusable components
- Leverage testing and other techniques for writing robust code

Leave a review - let other readers know what you think

Please share your thoughts on this book with others by leaving a review on the site that you bought it from. If you purchased the book from Amazon, please leave us an honest review on this book's Amazon page. This is vital so that other potential readers can see and use your unbiased opinion to make purchasing decisions, we can understand what our customers think about our products, and our authors can see your feedback on the title that they have worked with Packt to create. It will only take a few minutes of your time, but is valuable to other potential customers, our authors, and Packt. Thank you!

Index

W

weak reference 105, 107

World Wide Developers Conference (WWDC) 7, 123

Made in United States
North Haven, CT
19 January 2023